**VGM Professional Resumes Series**

THIRD EDITION

# RESUMES FOR

# HEALTH AND MEDICAL CAREERS

With Sample Cover Letters

DISCARD

## The Editors of VGM Career Books

*VGM Career Books*

*Chicago   New York   San Francisco   Lisbon   London   Madrid   Mexico City*
*Milan   New Delhi   San Juan   Seoul   Singapore   Sydney   Toronto*

**Library of Congress Cataloging-in-Publication Data**

Resumes for health and medical careers : with sample cover letters / the editors of VGM Career Books.—3rd ed.
        p.    cm. — (VGM professional resumes series)
    ISBN 0-07-141154-2
    1. Medical personnel—Vocational guidance.    2. Medicine—Vocational guidance.    3. Resumes (Employment)    4. Cover letters.    I. VGM Career Books (Firm).    II. Series.

R690.R48    2004
610.69—dc22                                             2003060129

2 3 4 5 6 7 8 9 0   QPD/QPD   2 1 0 9 8 7 6 5 4

ISBN 0-07-141154-2

McGraw-Hill books are available at special quantity discounts to use as premiums and sales promotions, or for use in corporate training programs. For more information, please write to the Director of Special Sales, Professional Publishing, McGraw-Hill, Two Penn Plaza, New York, NY 10121-2298. Or contact your local bookstore.

This book is printed on acid-free paper.

# Contents

# Introduction

Your resume is a piece of paper (or an electronic document) that serves to introduce you to the people who will eventually hire you. To write a thoughtful resume, you must thoroughly assess your personality, your accomplishments, and the skills you have acquired. The act of composing and submitting a resume also requires you to carefully consider the company or individual that might hire you. What are they looking for, and how can you meet their needs? This book shows you how to organize your personal information and experience into a concise and well-written resume, so that your qualifications and potential as an employee will be understood easily and quickly by a complete stranger.

Writing the resume is just one step in what can be a daunting job-search process, but it is an important element in the chain of events that will lead you to your new position. While you are probably a talented, bright, and charming person, your resume may not reflect these qualities. A poorly written resume can get you nowhere; a well-written resume can land you an interview and potentially a job. A good resume can even lead the interviewer to ask you questions that will allow you to talk about your strengths and highlight the skills you can bring to a prospective employer. Even a person with very little experience can find a good job if he or she is assisted by a thoughtful and polished resume.

Lengthy, typewritten resumes are a thing of the past. Today, employers do not have the time or the patience for verbose documents; they look for tightly composed, straightforward, action-based resumes. Although a one-page resume is the norm, a two-page resume may be warranted if you have had extensive job experience or have changed careers and truly need the space to properly position yourself. If, after careful editing, you still need more than one page to present yourself, it's acceptable to use a second page. A crowded resume that's hard to read would be the worst of your choices.

Distilling your work experience, education, and interests into such a small space requires preparation and thought. This book takes you step-by-step through the process of crafting an effective resume that will stand out in today's competitive marketplace. It serves as a workbook and a place to write down your experiences, while also including the techniques you'll need to pull all the necessary elements together. In the following pages, you'll find many examples of resumes that are specific to your area of interest. Study them for inspiration and find what appeals to you. There are a variety of ways to organize and present your information; inside, you'll find several that will be suitable to your needs. Good luck landing the job of your dreams!

# Chapter 1

# *The Elements of an Effective Resume*

An effective resume is composed of information that employers are most interested in knowing about a prospective job applicant. This information is conveyed by a few essential elements. The following is a list of elements that are found in most resumes—some essential, some optional. Later in this chapter, we will further examine the role of each of these elements in the makeup of your resume.

- Heading

- Objective and/or Keyword Section

- Work Experience

- Education

- Honors

- Activities

- Certificates and Licenses

- Publications

- Professional Memberships

- Special Skills

- Personal Information

- References

The first step in preparing your resume is to gather information about yourself and your past accomplishments. Later you will refine this information, rewrite it using effective language, and organize it into an attractive layout. But first, let's take a look at each of these important elements individually so you can judge their appropriateness for your resume.

## Heading

Although the heading may seem to be the simplest section of your resume, be careful not to take it lightly. It is the first section your prospective employer will see, and it contains the information she or he will need to contact you. At the very least, the heading must contain your name, your home address, and, of course, a phone number where you can be reached easily.

In today's high-tech world, many of us have multiple ways that we can be contacted. You may list your E-mail address if you are reasonably sure the employer makes use of this form of communication. Keep in mind, however, that others may have access to your E-mail messages if you send them from an account provided by your current company. If this is a concern, do not list your work E-mail address on your resume. If you are able to take calls at your current place of business, you should include your work number, because most employers will attempt to contact you during typical business hours.

If you have voice mail or a reliable answering machine at home or at work, list its number in the heading and make sure your greeting is professional and clear. Always include at least one phone number in your heading, even if it is a temporary number, where a prospective employer can leave a message.

You might have a dozen different ways to be contacted, but you do not need to list all of them. Confine your numbers or addresses to those that are the easiest for the prospective employer to use and the simplest for you to retrieve.

## Objective

When seeking a specific career path, it is important to list a job or career objective on your resume. This statement helps employers know the direction you see yourself taking, so they can determine whether your goals are in line with those of their organization and the position available. Normally, an objective is one to two sentences long. Its contents will vary depending on your career field, goals, and personality. The objective can be specific or general, but it should always be to the point. See the sample resumes in this book for examples.

If you are planning to use this resume online, or you suspect your potential employer is likely to scan your resume, you will want to include a "keyword" in the objective. This allows a prospective employer, searching hundreds of resumes for a specific skill or position objective, to locate the keyword and find your resume. In essence, a keyword is what's "hot" in your particular field at a given time. It's a buzzword, a shorthand way of getting a particular message across at a glance. For example, if you are a lawyer, your objective might state your desire to work in the area of corporate litigation. In this case, someone searching for the keyword "corporate litigation" will pull up your resume and know that you want to plan, research, and present cases at trial on behalf of the corporation. If your objective states that you "desire a challenging position in systems design," the keyword is "systems design," an industry-specific, shorthand way of saying that you want to be involved in assessing the need for, acquiring, and implementing high-technology systems. These are keywords and every industry has them, so it's becoming more and more important to include a few in your resume. (You may need to conduct additional research to make sure you know what keywords are most likely to be used in your desired industry, profession, or situation.)

There are many resume and job-search sites online. Like most things in the online world, they vary a great deal in quality. Use your discretion. If you plan to apply for jobs online or advertise your availability this way, you will want to design a scannable resume. This type of resume uses a format that can be easily scanned into a computer and added to a database. Scanning allows a prospective employer to use keywords to quickly review each applicant's experience and skills, and (in the event that there are many candidates for the job) to keep your resume for future reference.

Many people find that it is worthwhile to create two or more versions of their basic resume. You may want an intricately designed resume on high-quality paper to mail or hand out *and* a resume that is designed to be scanned into a computer and saved on a database or an online job site. You can even create a resume in ASCII text to E-mail to prospective employers. For further information, you may wish to refer to the *Guide to Internet Job Searching*, by Frances Roehm and Margaret Dikel, updated and published every other year by VGM Career Books, a division of the McGraw-Hill Companies. This excellent book contains helpful and detailed information about formatting a resume for Internet use. To get you started, in Chapter 3 we have included a list of things to keep in mind when creating electronic resumes.

Although it is usually a good idea to include an objective, in some cases this element is not necessary. The goal of the objective statement is to provide the employer with an idea of where you see yourself going in the field. However, if you are uncertain of the exact nature of the job you seek, including an objective that is too specific could result in your not being considered for a host of perfectly acceptable positions. If you decide not to use an objective heading in your resume, you should definitely incorporate the information that would be conveyed in the objective into your cover letter.

## Work Experience

Work experience is arguably the most important element of them all. Unless you are a recent graduate or former homemaker with little or no relevant work experience, your current and former positions will provide the central focus of the resume. You will want this section to be as complete and carefully constructed as possible. By thoroughly examining your work experience, you can get to the heart of your accomplishments and present them in a way that demonstrates and highlights your qualifications.

If you are just entering the workforce, your resume will probably focus on your education, but you should also include information on your work or volunteer experiences. Although you will have less information about work experience than a person who has held multiple positions or is advanced in his or her career, the amount of information is not what is most important in this section. How the information is presented and what it says about you as a worker and a person is what really counts.

As you create this section of your resume, remember the need for accuracy. Include all the necessary information about each of your jobs, including your job title, dates of employment, name of your employer, city, state, responsibilities, special projects you handled, and accomplishments. Be sure to list only accomplishments for which you were directly responsible. And don't be alarmed if you haven't participated in or worked on special projects, because this section may not be relevant to certain jobs.

The most common way to list your work experience is in *reverse chronological order*. In other words, start with your most recent job and work your way backward. This way, your prospective employer sees your current (and often most important) position before considering your past employment. Your most recent position, if it's the most important in terms of responsibilities and relevance to the job for which you are applying, should also be the one that includes the most information as compared to your previous positions.

Even if the work itself seems unrelated to your proposed career path, you should list any job or experience that will help "sell" your talents. If you were promoted or given greater responsibilities or commendations, be sure to mention the fact.

The following worksheet is provided to help you organize your experiences in the working world. It will also serve as an excellent resource to refer to when updating your resume in the future.

## WORK EXPERIENCE

Job One:

Job Title _____

Dates _____

Employer _____

City, State _____

Major Duties _____

_____

_____

_____

_____

_____

_____

_____

_____

_____

Special Projects _____

_____

_____

_____

Accomplishments _____

_____

_____

_____

_____

_____

**Job Two:**

Job Title _____

Dates _____

Employer _____

City, State _____

Major Duties _____

_____

_____

_____

_____

_____

_____

_____

_____

Special Projects _____

_____

_____

_____

Accomplishments _____

_____

_____

_____

_____

_____

_____

_____

_____

**Job Three:**


Job Title _____

Dates _____

Employer _____

City, State _____

Major Duties _____

_____

_____

_____

_____

_____

_____

_____

Special Projects _____

_____

_____

_____

Accomplishments _____

_____

_____

_____

_____

_____

_____

_____

_____

**Job Four:**


Job Title _____

Dates _____

Employer _____

City, State _____

Major Duties _____

_____

_____

_____

_____

_____

_____

_____

Special Projects _____

_____

_____

_____

Accomplishments _____

_____

_____

_____

_____

_____

_____

_____

_____

## Education

Education is usually the second most important element of a resume. Your educational background is often a deciding factor in an employer's decision to interview you. Highlight your accomplishments in school as much as you did those accomplishments at work. If you are looking for your first professional job, your education or life experience will be your greatest assets because your related work experience will be minimal. In this case, the education section becomes the most important means of selling yourself.

Include in this section all the degrees or certificates you have received; your major or area of concentration; all of the honors you earned; and any relevant activities you participated in, organized, or chaired. Again, list your most recent schooling first. If you have completed graduate-level work, begin with that and work your way back through your undergraduate education. If you have completed college, you generally should not list your high school experience; do so only if you earned special honors, you had a grade point average that was much better than the norm, or this was your highest level of education.

If you have completed a large number of credit hours in a subject that may be relevant to the position you are seeking but did not obtain a degree, you may wish to list the hours or classes you completed. Keep in mind, however, that you may be asked to explain why you did not finish the program. If you are currently in school, list the degree, certificate, or license you expect to obtain and the projected date of completion.

The following worksheet will help you gather the information you need for this section of your resume.

**EDUCATION**

School One _____

Major or Area of Concentration _____

Degree _____

Dates _____

School Two _____

Major or Area of Concentration _____

Degree _____

Dates _____

## Honors

If you include an honors section in your resume, you should highlight any awards, honors, or memberships in honorary societies that you have received. (You may also incorporate this information into your education section.) Often, the honors are academic in nature, but this section also may be used for special achievements in sports, clubs, or other school activities. Always include the name of the organization awarding the honor and the date(s) received. Use the following worksheet to help you gather your information.

### HONORS

Honor One _____

Awarding Organization _____

Date(s) _____

Honor Two _____

Awarding Organization _____

Date(s) _____

Honor Three _____

Awarding Organization _____

Date(s) _____

Honor Four _____

Awarding Organization _____

Date(s) _____

Honor Five _____

Awarding Organization _____

Date(s) _____

## Activities

Perhaps you have been active in different organizations or clubs; often an employer will look at such involvement as evidence of initiative, dedication, and good social skills. Examples of your ability to take a leading role in a group should be included on a resume, if you can provide them. The activities section of your resume should present neighborhood and community activities, volunteer positions, and so forth. In general, you may want to avoid listing any organization whose name indicates the race, creed, sex, age, marital status, sexual orientation, or nation of origin of its members because this could expose you to discrimination. Use the following worksheet to list the specifics of your activities.

## ACTIVITIES

Organization/Activity _____

Accomplishments _____

_____

_____

Organization/Activity _____

Accomplishments _____

_____

_____

Organization/Activity _____

Accomplishments _____

_____

_____

As your work experience grows through the years, your school activities and honors will carry less weight and be emphasized less in your resume. Eventually, you will probably list only your degree and any major honors received. As time goes by, your job performance and the experience you've gained become the most important elements in your resume, which should change to reflect this.

## Certificates and Licenses

If your chosen career path requires specialized training, you may already have certificates or licenses. You should list these if the job you are seeking requires them and you, of course, have acquired them. If you have applied for a license but have not yet received it, use the phrase "application pending."

License requirements vary by state. If you have moved or are planning to relocate to another state, check with that state's board or licensing agency for all licensing requirements.

Always make sure that all of the information you list is completely accurate. Locate copies of your certificates and licenses, and check the exact date and name of the accrediting agency. Use the following worksheet to organize the necessary information.

## CERTIFICATES AND LICENSES

Name of License _____

Licensing Agency _____

Date Issued _____

Name of License _____

Licensing Agency _____

Date Issued _____

Name of License _____

Licensing Agency _____

Date Issued _____

## Publications

Some professions strongly encourage or even require that you publish. If you have written, coauthored, or edited any books, articles, professional papers, or works of a similar nature that pertain to your field, you will definitely want to include this element. Remember to list the date of publication and the publisher's name, and specify whether you were the sole author or a coauthor. Book, magazine, or journal titles are generally italicized, while the titles of articles within a larger publication appear in quotes. (Check with your reference librarian for more about the appropriate way to present this information.) For scientific or research papers, you will need to give the date, place, and audience to whom the paper was presented.

Use the following worksheet to help you gather the necessary information about your publications.

## PUBLICATIONS

Title and Type (Note, Article, etc.) _____

Title of Publication (Journal, Book, etc.) _____

Publisher _____

Date Published _____

Title and Type (Note, Article, etc.) _____

Title of Publication (Journal, Book, etc.) _____

Publisher _____

Date Published _____

Title and Type (Note, Article, etc.) _____

Title of Publication (Journal, Book, etc.) _____

Publisher _____

Date Published _____

## Professional Memberships

Another potential element in your resume is a section listing professional memberships. Use this section to describe your involvement in professional associations, unions, and similar organizations. It is to your advantage to list any professional memberships that pertain to the job you are seeking. Many employers see your membership as representative of your desire to stay up-to-date and connected in your field. Include the dates of your involvement and whether you took part in any special activities or held any offices within the organization. Use the following worksheet to organize your information.

### PROFESSIONAL MEMBERSHIPS

Name of Organization _____

Office(s) Held_____

Activities _____

Dates _____

Name of Organization _____

Office(s) Held_____

Activities _____

Dates _____

Name of Organization _____

Office(s) Held_____

Activities _____

Dates _____

Name of Organization _____

Office(s) Held_____

Activities _____

Dates _____

## Special Skills

The special skills section of your resume is the place to mention any special abilities you have that relate to the job you are seeking. You can use this element to present certain talents or experiences that are not necessarily a part of your education or work experience. Common examples include fluency in a foreign language, extensive travel abroad, or knowledge of a particular computer application. "Special skills" can encompass a wide range of talents, and this section can be used creatively. However, for each skill you list, you should be able to describe how it would be a direct asset in the type of work you're seeking because employers may ask just that in an interview. If you can't think of a way to do this, it may be extraneous information.

## Personal Information

Some people include personal information on their resumes. This is generally not recommended, but you might wish to include it if you think that something in your personal life, such as a hobby or talent, has some bearing on the position you are seeking. This type of information is often referred to at the beginning of an interview, when it may be used as an "icebreaker." Of course, personal information regarding your age, marital status, race, religion, or sexual orientation should never appear on your resume as *personal information*. It should be given only in the context of memberships and activities, and only when doing so would not expose you to discrimination.

## References

References are not usually given on the resume itself, but a prospective employer needs to know that you have references who may be contacted if necessary. All you need to include is a single sentence at the end of the resume: "References are available upon request," or even simply, "References available." Have a reference list ready—your interviewer may ask to see it! Contact each person on the list ahead of time to see whether it is all right for you to use him or her as a reference. This way, the person has a chance to think about what to say *before* the call occurs. This helps ensure that you will obtain the best reference possible.

# Chapter 2

# Writing Your Resume

Now that you have gathered the information for each section of your resume, it's time to write it out in a way that will get the attention of the reviewer—hopefully, your future employer! The language you use in your resume will affect its success, so you must be careful and conscientious. Translate the facts you have gathered into the active, precise language of resume writing. You will be aiming for a resume that keeps the reader's interest and highlights your accomplishments in a concise and effective way.

Resume writing is unlike any other form of writing. Although your seventh-grade composition teacher would not approve, the rules of punctuation and sentence building are often completely ignored. Instead, you should try for a functional, direct writing style that focuses on the use of verbs and other words that imply action on your part. Writing with action words and strong verbs characterizes you to potential employers as an energetic, active person, someone who completes tasks and achieves results from his or her work. Resumes that do not make use of action words can sound passive and stale. These resumes are not effective and do not get the attention of any employer, no matter how qualified the applicant. Choose words that display your strengths and demonstrate your initiative. The following list of commonly used verbs will help you create a strong resume:

| | |
|---|---|
| administered | assembled |
| advised | assumed responsibility |
| analyzed | billed |
| arranged | built |

| | |
|---|---|
| carried out | inspected |
| channeled | interviewed |
| collected | introduced |
| communicated | invented |
| compiled | maintained |
| completed | managed |
| conducted | met with |
| contacted | motivated |
| contracted | negotiated |
| coordinated | operated |
| counseled | orchestrated |
| created | ordered |
| cut | organized |
| designed | oversaw |
| determined | performed |
| developed | planned |
| directed | prepared |
| dispatched | presented |
| distributed | produced |
| documented | programmed |
| edited | published |
| established | purchased |
| expanded | recommended |
| functioned as | recorded |
| gathered | reduced |
| handled | referred |
| hired | represented |
| implemented | researched |
| improved | reviewed |

| | |
|---|---|
| saved | supervised |
| screened | taught |
| served as | tested |
| served on | trained |
| sold | typed |
| suggested | wrote |

Let's look at two examples that differ only in their writing style. The first resume section is ineffective because it does not use action words to accent the applicant's work experiences.

## WORK EXPERIENCE
### *Regional Sales Manager*

Manager of sales representatives from seven states. Manager of twelve food chain accounts in the East. In charge of the sales force's planned selling toward specific goals. Supervisor and trainer of new sales representatives. Consulting for customers in the areas of inventory management and quality control.

*Special Projects*: Coordinator and sponsor of annual food-industry sales seminar.

*Accomplishments*: Monthly regional volume went up 25 percent during my tenure while, at the same time, a proper sales/cost ratio was maintained. Customer-company relations were improved.

In the following paragraph, we have rewritten the same section using action words. Notice how the tone has changed. It now sounds stronger and more active. This person accomplished goals and really *did* things.

## WORK EXPERIENCE
### *Regional Sales Manager*

Managed sales representatives from seven states. Oversaw twelve food chain accounts in the eastern United States. Directed the sales force in planned selling toward specific goals. Supervised and trained new sales representatives. Counseled customers in the areas of inventory management and quality control. Coordinated and sponsored the annual Food Industry Seminar. Increased monthly regional volume 25 percent and helped to improve customer-company relations during my tenure.

One helpful way to construct the work experience section is to make use of your actual job descriptions—the written duties and expectations your employers had for a person in your current or former position. Job descriptions are rarely written in proper resume language, so you will have to rework them, but they do include much of the information necessary to create this section of your resume. If you have access to job descriptions for your former positions, you can use the details to construct an action-oriented paragraph. Often, your human resources department can provide a job description for your current position.

The following is an example of a typical human resources job description, followed by a rewritten version of the same description employing action words and specific details about the job. Again, pay attention to the style of writing instead of the content, as the details of your own experience will be unique.

**WORK EXPERIENCE**
*Public Administrator I*

*Responsibilities*: Coordinate and direct public services to meet the needs of the nation, state, or community. Analyze problems; work with special committees and public agencies; recommend solutions to governing bodies.

*Aptitudes and Skills*: Ability to relate to and communicate with people; solve complex problems through analysis; plan, organize, and implement policies and programs. Knowledge of political systems, financial management, personnel administration, program evaluation, and organizational theory.

**WORK EXPERIENCE**
*Public Administrator I*

Wrote pamphlets and conducted discussion groups to inform citizens of legislative processes and consumer issues. Organized and supervised 25 interviewers. Trained interviewers in effective communication skills.

After you have written out your resume, you are ready to begin the next important step: assembly and layout.

# Chapter 3

# Assembly and Layout

At this point, you've gathered all the necessary information for your resume and rewritten it in language that will impress your potential employers. Your next step is to assemble the sections in a logical order and lay them out on the page neatly and attractively to achieve the desired effect: getting the interview.

## Assembly

The order of the elements in a resume makes a difference in its overall effect. Clearly, you would not want to bury your name and address somewhere in the middle of the resume. Nor would you want to lead with a less important section, such as special skills. Put the elements in an order that stresses your most important accomplishments and the things that will be most appealing to your potential employer. For example, if you are new to the workforce, you will want the reviewer to read about your education and life skills before any part-time jobs you may have held for short durations. On the other hand, if you have been gainfully employed for several years and currently hold an important position in your company, you should list your work accomplishments ahead of your educational information, which has become less pertinent with time.

Certain things should always be included in your resume, but others are optional. The following list shows you which are which. You might want to use it as a checklist to be certain that you have included all of the necessary information.

| **Essential** | **Optional** |
|---|---|
| Name | Cellular Phone Number |
| Address | Pager Number |
| Phone Number | E-Mail Address or Website Address |
| Work Experience | Voice Mail Number |
| Education | Job Objective |
| References Phrase | Honors |
| | Special Skills |
| | Publications |
| | Professional Memberships |
| | Activities |
| | Certificates and Licenses |
| | Personal Information |
| | Graphics |
| | Photograph |

Your choice of optional sections depends on your own background and employment needs. Always use information that will put you in a favorable light—unless it's absolutely essential, avoid anything that will prompt the interviewer to ask questions about your weaknesses or something else that could be unflattering. Make sure your information is accurate and truthful. If your honors are impressive, include them in the resume. If your activities in school demonstrate talents that are necessary for the job you are seeking, allow space for a section on activities. If you are applying for a position that requires ornamental illustration, you may want to include border illustrations or graphics that demonstrate your talents in this area. If you are answering an advertisement for a job that requires certain physical traits, a photo of yourself might be appropriate. A person applying for a job as a computer programmer would *not* include a photo as part of his or her resume. Each resume is unique, just as each person is unique.

# Types of Resumes

So far we have focused on the most common type of resume—the *reverse chronological* resume—in which your most recent job is listed first. This is the type of resume usually preferred by those who have to read a large number of resumes, and it is by far the most popular and widely circulated. However, this style of presentation may not be the most effective way to highlight *your* skills and accomplishments.

For example, if you are reentering the workforce after many years or are trying to change career fields, the *functional* resume may work best. This type of resume puts the focus on your achievements instead of the sequence of your work history. In the functional resume, your experience is presented through your general accomplishments and the skills you have developed in your working life.

A functional resume is assembled from the same information you gathered in Chapter 1. The main difference lies in how you organize the information. Essentially, the work experience section is divided in two, with your job duties and accomplishments constituting one section and your employers' names, cities, and states; your positions; and the dates employed making up the other. Place the first section near the top of your resume, just below your job objective (if used), and call it *Accomplishments* or *Achievements*. The second section, containing the bare essentials of your work history, should come after the accomplishments section and can be called *Employment History*, since it is a chronological overview of your former jobs.

The other sections of your resume remain the same. The work experience section is the only one affected in the functional format. By placing the section that focuses on your achievements at the beginning, you draw attention to these achievements. This puts less emphasis on whom you worked for and when, and more on what you did and what you are capable of doing.

If you are changing careers, the emphasis on skills and achievements is important. The identities of previous employers (who aren't part of your new career field) need to be downplayed. A functional resume can help accomplish this task. If you are reentering the workforce after a long absence, a functional resume is the obvious choice. And if you lack full-time work experience, you will need to draw attention away from this fact and put the focus on your skills and abilities. You may need to highlight your volunteer activities and part-time work. Education may also play a more important role in your resume.

The type of resume that is right for you will depend on your personal circumstances. It may be helpful to create both types and then compare them. Which one presents you in the best light? Examples of both types of resumes are included in this book. Use the sample resumes in Chapter 5 to help you decide on the content, presentation, and look of your own resume.

## Resume or Curriculum Vitae?

A curriculum vitae (CV) is a longer, more detailed synopsis of your professional history, which generally runs three or more pages in length. It includes a summary of your educational and academic background as well as teaching and research experience, publications, presentations, awards, honors, affiliations, and other details. Because the purpose of the CV is different from that of the resume, many of the rules we've discussed thus far involving style and length do not apply.

A curriculum vitae is used primarily for admissions applications to graduate or professional schools, independent consulting in a variety of settings, proposals for fellowships or grants, or applications for positions in academia. As with a resume, you may need different versions of a CV for different types of positions. You should only send a CV when one is specifically requested by an employer or institution.

Like a resume, your CV should include your name, contact information, education, skills and experience. In addition to the basics, a CV includes research and teaching experience, publications, grants and fellowships, professional associations and licenses, awards, and other information relevant to the position for which you are applying. You can follow the advice presented thus far to gather and organize your personal information.

## Special Tips for Electronic Resumes

Because there are many details to consider in writing a resume that will be posted or transmitted on the Internet, or one that will be scanned into a computer when it is received, we suggest that you refer to the *Guide to Internet Job Searching*, by Frances Roehm and Margaret Dikel, as previously mentioned. However, here are some brief, general guidelines to follow if you expect your resume to be scanned into a computer.

- Use standard fonts in which none of the letters touch.

- Keep in mind that underlining, italics, and fancy scripts may not scan well.

- Use boldface and capitalization to set off elements. Again, make sure letters don't touch. Leave at least a quarter inch between lines of type.

- Keep information and elements at the left margin. Centering, columns, and even indenting may change when the resume is optically scanned.

- Do not use any lines, boxes, or graphics.

- Place the most important information at the top of the first page. If you use two pages, put "Page 1 of 2" at the bottom of the first page and put your name and "Page 2 of 2" at the top of the second page.

- List each telephone number on its own line in the header.

- Use multiple keywords or synonyms for what you do to make sure your qualifications will be picked up if a prospective employer is searching for them. Use nouns that are keywords for your profession.

- Be descriptive in your titles. For example, don't just use "assistant"; use "legal office assistant."

- Make sure the contrast between print and paper is good. Use a high-quality laser printer and white or very light colored 8½-by-11-inch paper.

- Mail a high-quality laser print or an excellent copy. Do not fold or use staples, as this might interfere with scanning. You may, however, use paper clips.

In addition to creating a resume that works well for scanning, you may want to have a resume that can be E-mailed to reviewers. Because you may not know what word processing application the recipient uses, the best format to use is ASCII text. (ASCII stands for "American Standard Code for Information Exchange.") It allows people with very different software platforms to exchange and understand information. (E-mail operates on this principle.) ASCII is a simple, text-only language, which means you can include only simple text. There can be no use of boldface, italics, or even paragraph indentations.

To create an ASCII resume, just use your normal word processing program; when finished, save it as a "text only" document. You will find this option under the "save" or "save as" command. Here is a list of things to *avoid* when crafting your electronic resume:

- Tabs. Use your space bar. Tabs will not work.

- Any special characters, such as mathematical symbols.

- Word wrap. Use hard returns (the return key) to make line breaks.

- Centering or other formatting. Align everything at the left margin.

- Bold or italic fonts. Everything will be converted to plain text when you save the file as a "text only" document.

Check carefully for any mistakes before you save the document as a text file. Spellcheck and proofread it several times; then ask someone with a keen eye to go over it again for you. Remember: the key is to keep it simple. Any attempt to make this resume pretty or decorative may result in a resume that is confusing and hard to read. After you have saved the document, you can cut and paste it into an E-mail or onto a website.

## Layout for a Paper Resume

A great deal of care—and much more formatting—is necessary to achieve an attractive layout for your paper resume. There is no single appropriate layout that applies to every resume, but there are a few basic rules to follow in putting your resume on paper:

- Leave a comfortable margin on the sides, top, and bottom of the page (usually one to one and a half inches).

- Use appropriate spacing between the sections (two to three line spaces are usually adequate).

- Be consistent in the type of headings you use for different sections of your resume. For example, if you capitalize the heading EMPLOY-MENT HISTORY, don't use initial capitals and underlining for a section of equal importance, such as Education.

- Do not use more than one font in your resume. Stay consistent by choosing a font that is fairly standard and easy to read, and don't change it for different sections. Beware of the tendency to try to make your resume original by choosing fancy type styles; your resume may end up looking unprofessional instead of creative. Unless you are in a very creative and artistic field, you should almost always stick with tried-and-true type styles like Times New Roman and Palatino, which are often used in business writing. In the area of resume styles, conservative is usually the best way to go.

**CHRONOLOGICAL RESUME**

# ALEXANDER CLARKE

**85 Starview Lane • Kalamazoo, MI 49002**
**Home: (616) 555-6812**
**Cellular: (616) 555-3448**

## *Career Objective*

*Position as a health care administrator in a hospital or clinic serving the mentally handicapped.*

## *Education*

Bachelor of Science, June 1995
Psychology Major, Accounting Minor
Ball State University, Muncie, Indiana

- 3.49 G.P.A.
- Kappa Delta Tau (Honor Society in Psychology)
- Dean's List (5 times)

## *Professional Experience*

**Managing Director, Craig L. Turner Clinic**
**January 2002 – present**

Responsible for all aspects of operation of the clinic including financial planning, personnel, and cost control. Also, coordinate all nursing and medical activities.

**Assistant Director, Kelly Hospital**
**June 1999 – December 2001**

Managed medical record department, inpatient admittance, and budget planning.

**Administrative Supervisor, Muncie Community Hospitals**
**July 1995 – May 1999**

Trained personnel, hired staff, and administered educational services.

*References Available*

**FUNCTIONAL RESUME**

# Michael Martinez

455 Lilac Lane • Mooresville, IN 46158 • Martinez1@xxx.com • 317-555-7892

## Education

B.A. from Hanover College, Hanover, Indiana, 1999
- Magna Cum Laude, 3.93 G.P.A.
- Highest Departmental Honors in Chemistry, 4.0 G.P.A.
- All-American Football Lineman, Co-Captain in Senior Year
- Four Varsity Letters
- National Football Foundation and Hall of Fame Scholar Athlete Award

M.D. from Indiana University School of Medicine, Indianapolis, Indiana, 2003
- Honors Marks: Gross Anatomy and Systemic Pathology
- Clerkships in Pediatrics and Neuroscience

## Research Experience

Senior Research Thesis in Department of Chemistry, Hanover College, 2001–2002
Robert M. Gibbons, Ph.D.
Associate Professor of Chemistry, Hanover, Indiana

Summer Research at St. Vincent's Sports Clinic, Indianapolis, Indiana, 2001
Andrew M. Sporn, M.D.
Director of Research and Development

## Publications

**1.** Gibbons, R. M., and M. Martinez: "Forward and Reverse Rate Constants in the Diel-Alder Reaction." Senior Research Thesis File, Duggan Library, Hanover College, Hanover, Indiana, May 1999.

**2.** Sporn, A., M. Jones, M. Martinez, and K. L. Jones: "Isolated Fractures of the Tibial Eminence in Adults Associated with Anterior Laxity." *Journal of Sports Medicine*, Spring 2002.

## Medical Illustrations

**1.** Kingsman, M. A.: "Neurovascular Injuries in the Wrists and Hands of Athletes," *Clinics in Sports Medicine*, Vol. 9, No. 2, April 2001.

**2.** Michaels, J. B., and M. E. Tory: "Meniscal Transplantation," Presentation, Duke University School of Medicine, Durham, North Carolina, May 2002.

## Work Experience

Extern, Henry County Memorial Hospital, New Castle, Indiana, 2001–2002
Summer Research Intern, Methodist Sports Clinic, Indianapolis, Indiana, 2001

- Always try to fit your resume on one page. If you are having trouble with this, you may be trying to say too much. Edit out any repetitive or unnecessary information, and shorten descriptions of earlier jobs where possible. Ask a friend you trust for feedback on what seems unnecessary or unimportant. For example, you may have included too many optional sections. Today, with the prevalence of the personal computer as a tool, there is no excuse for a poorly laid out resume. Experiment with variations until you are pleased with the result.

Remember that a resume is not an autobiography. Too much information will only get in the way. The more compact your resume, the easier it will be to review. If a person who is swamped with resumes looks at yours, catches the main points, and then calls you for an interview to fill in some of the details, your resume has already accomplished its task. A clear and concise resume makes for a happy reader and a good impression.

There are times when, despite extensive editing, the resume simply cannot fit on one page. In this case, the resume should be laid out on two pages in such a way that neither clarity nor appearance is compromised. Each page of a two-page resume should be marked clearly: the first should indicate "Page 1 of 2," and the second should include your name and the page number, for example, "Julia Ramirez—Page 2 of 2." The pages should then be stapled together. You may use a smaller font (in the same font as the body of your resume) for the page numbers. Place them at the bottom of page one and the top of page two. Again, spend the time now to experiment with the layout until you find one that looks good to you.

Always show your final layout to other people and ask them what they like or dislike about it, and what impresses them most when they read your resume. Make sure that their responses are the same as what you want to elicit from your prospective employer. If they aren't the same, you should continue to make changes until the necessary information is emphasized.

## Proofreading

After you have finished typing the master copy of your resume and before you have it copied or printed, thoroughly check it for typing and spelling errors. Do not place all your trust in your computer's spellcheck function. Use an old editing trick and read the whole resume backward—start at the end and read it right to left and bottom to top. This can help you see the small errors or inconsistencies that are easy to overlook. Take time to do it right because a single error on a document this important can cause the reader to judge your attention to detail in a harsh light.

Have several people look at the finished resume just in case you've missed an error. Don't try to take a shortcut; not having an unbiased set of eyes examine your resume now could mean embarrassment later. Even experienced editors can easily overlook their own errors. Be thorough and conscientious with your proofreading so your first impression is a perfect one.

We have included the following rules of capitalization and punctuation to assist you in the final stage of creating your resume. Remember that resumes often require use of a shorthand style of writing that may include sentences without periods and other stylistic choices that break the standard rules of grammar. Be consistent in each section and throughout the whole resume with your choices.

## RULES OF CAPITALIZATION

- Capitalize proper nouns, such as names of schools, colleges, and universities; names of companies; and brand names of products.

- Capitalize major words in the names and titles of books, tests, and articles that appear in the body of your resume.

- Capitalize words in major section headings of your resume.

- Do not capitalize words just because they seem important.

- When in doubt, consult a manual of style such as *Words into Type* (Prentice-Hall) or *The Chicago Manual of Style* (The University of Chicago Press). Your local library can help you locate these and other reference books. Many computer programs also have grammar help sections.

## RULES OF PUNCTUATION

- Use commas to separate words in a series.

- Use a semicolon to separate series of words that already include commas within the series. (For an example, see the first rule of capitalization.)

- Use a semicolon to separate independent clauses that are not joined by a conjunction.

- Use a period to end a sentence.

- Use a colon to show that examples or details follow that will expand or amplify the preceding phrase.

- Avoid the use of dashes.

- Avoid the use of brackets.

- If you use any punctuation in an unusual way in your resume, be consistent in its use.

- Whenever you are uncertain, consult a style manual.

## Putting Your Resume in Print

You will need to buy high-quality paper for your printer before you print your finished resume. Regular office paper is not good enough for resumes; the reviewer will probably think it looks flimsy and cheap. Go to an office supply store or copy shop and select a high-quality bond paper that will make a good first impression. Select colors like white, off-white, or possibly a light gray. In some industries, a pastel may be acceptable, but be sure the color and feel of the paper makes a subtle, positive statement about you. Nothing in the choice of paper should be loud or unprofessional.

If your computer printer does not reproduce your resume properly and produces smudged or stuttered type, either ask to borrow a friend's or take your disk (or a clean original) to a printer or copy shop for high-quality copying. If you anticipate needing a large number of copies, taking your resume to a copy shop or a printer is probably the best choice.

Hold a sheet of your unprinted bond paper up to the light. If it has a watermark, you will want to point this out to the person helping you with copies; the printing should be done so that the reader can read the print and see the watermark the right way up. Check each copy for smudges or streaks. This is the time to be a perfectionist—the results of your careful preparation will be well worth it.

# *The Cover Letter*

Once your resume has been assembled, laid out, and printed to your satisfaction, the next and final step before distribution is to write your cover letter. Though there may be instances where you deliver your resume in person, you will usually send it through the mail or online. Resumes sent through the mail always need an accompanying letter that briefly introduces you and your resume. The purpose of the cover letter is to get a potential employer to read your resume, just as the purpose of the resume is to get that same potential employer to call you for an interview.

Like your resume, your cover letter should be clean, neat, and direct. A cover letter usually includes the following information:

1. Your name and address (unless it already appears on your personal letterhead) and your phone number(s); see item 7.

2. The date.

3. The name and address of the person and company to whom you are sending your resume.

4. The salutation ("Dear Mr." or "Dear Ms." followed by the person's last name, or "To Whom It May Concern" if you are answering a blind ad).

5. An opening paragraph explaining why you are writing (for example, in response to an ad, as a follow-up to a previous meeting, at the suggestion of someone you both know) and indicating that you are interested in whatever job is being offered.

6. One or more paragraphs that tell why you want to work for the company and what qualifications and experiences you can bring to the position. This is a good place to mention some detail about

that particular company that makes you want to work for them; this shows that you have done some research before applying.

7. A final paragraph that closes the letter and invites the reviewer to contact you for an interview. This can be a good place to tell the potential employer which method would be best to use when contacting you. Be sure to give the correct phone number and a good time to reach you, if that is important. You may mention here that your references are available upon request.

8. The closing ("Sincerely" or "Yours truly") followed by your signature in a dark ink, with your name typed under it.

Your cover letter should include all of this information and be no longer than one page in length. The language used should be polite, businesslike, and to the point. Don't attempt to tell your life story in the cover letter; a long and cluttered letter will serve only to annoy the reader. Remember that you need to mention only a few of your accomplishments and skills in the cover letter. The rest of your information is available in your resume. If your cover letter is a success, your resume will be read and all pertinent information reviewed by your prospective employer.

## Producing the Cover Letter

Cover letters should always be individualized because they are always written to specific individuals and companies. Never use a form letter for your cover letter or copy it as you would a resume. Each cover letter should be unique, and as personal and lively as possible. (Of course, once you have written and rewritten your first cover letter until you are satisfied with it, you can certainly use similar wording in subsequent letters. You may want to save a template on your computer for future reference.) Keep a hard copy of each cover letter so you know exactly what you wrote in each one.

There are sample cover letters in Chapter 6. Use them as models or for ideas of how to assemble and lay out your own cover letters. Remember that every letter is unique and depends on the particular circumstances of the individual writing it and the job for which he or she is applying.

After you have written your cover letter, proofread it as thoroughly as you did your resume. Again, spelling or punctuation errors are a sure sign of carelessness, and you don't want that to be a part of your first impression on a prospective employer. This is no time to trust your spellcheck function. Even after going through a spelling and grammar check, your cover letter should be carefully proofread by at least one other person.

Print the cover letter on the same quality bond paper you used for your resume. Remember to sign it, using a good, dark-ink pen. Handle the letter and resume carefully to avoid smudging or wrinkling, and mail them together in an appropriately sized envelope. Many stores sell matching envelopes to coordinate with your choice of bond paper.

Keep an accurate record of all resumes you send out and the results of each mailing. This record can be kept on your computer, in a calendar or notebook, or on file cards. Knowing when a resume is likely to have been received will keep you on track as you make follow-up phone calls.

About a week after mailing resumes and cover letters to potential employers, contact them by telephone. Confirm that your resume arrived and ask whether an interview might be possible. Be sure to record the name of the person you spoke to and any other information you gleaned from the conversation. It is wise to treat the person answering the phone with a great deal of respect; sometimes the assistant or receptionist has the ear of the person doing the hiring.

You should make a great impression with the strong, straightforward resume and personalized cover letter you have just created. We wish you every success in securing the career of your dreams!

# *Sample Resumes*

This chapter contains dozens of sample resumes for people pursuing a wide variety of health and medical careers.

There are many different styles of resumes and curricula vitae in terms of graphic layout and presentation of information. These samples also represent people with varying amounts of education and experience. Use these samples to model your own resume after. Choose one resume, or borrow elements from several different resumes to help you construct your own.

# Franklin Wu

5391 Southward Plaza
Walnut Creek, CA 94596
(510) 555-9008
Frank.Wu@xxx.com

## Job Objective

To obtain a position as a management optician in a fast-paced retail store.

## Education

Graduated Hayward Community College in Hayward, CA
June 2001

Graduated North Central High School in Chicago, IL
June 1999

## Work Experience

Great Spectacles, Walnut Creek, CA
2001 - present
Management Optician

Valley Vision, Pleasanton, CA
1999 - 2001
Sales Associate

## Special Skills

- Excellent customer service skills
- Fashion styling experience
- Knowledge of adjustment, repair, and fitting of glasses and contact lenses

## Certification

American Board of Optometry Certificate

## Seminars

Cal-Q Optics to prepare for licensing, 2003
Opti-Fair (annual three-day seminars)

## References

George Jones, O.D.
Great Spectacles, (510) 555-8941

Maria Lazar, Optician
Valley Vision, (510) 555-3726

# P A T R I C I A   W H I T E

**987 West 44th Street • Cheyenne, WY 82001**
**(307) 555-9872 • PKWhite@xxx.com**

## PROFESSIONAL OBJECTIVE
To obtain a position that presents an opportunity to demonstrate superior managerial ability and administrative decision-making skills in a nursing home environment.

## SUMMARY OF QUALIFICATIONS
• High degree of motivation
• Ability and patience to train and develop office/professional staff
• Thorough knowledge of Microsoft Office including Word and Excel, Lotus 1-2-3, and IBM 38 10-key by touch
• Dictation

## EDUCATION
University of Wyoming, B.A. Business
Laramie, Wyoming

## EXPERIENCE
Assistant Director
Longview Manor, Cheyenne, WY
April 2001 – present

Business Manager
Mountain Top Nursing Home, Cheyenne, WY
October 1998 – April 2001

## REFERENCES
Excellent professional and personal references are available upon request.

# Hanna Mayers, M.D.

| **Home Address** | **Work Address** |
|---|---|
| 111 Barclay | NICU |
| Cincinnati, OH 45219 | Henry Wilkins Hospital |
| 513-555-7987 | 2799 North Street |
| HannaMayers@xxx.com | Cincinnati, OH 45219 |
| Pager: 513-555-7659 | 513-555-8811 |

## *Specialty*

Neonatology

## *Education*

**Undergraduate**
Notre Dame University, South Bend, IN
1983 - 1987
Degree: B.S.
Graduated Magna Cum Laude

**Graduate**
Indiana University, Bloomington, IN
1987 - 1988
Degree: M.B.A., concentration on Finance
Graduated Magna Cum Laude

**Medical School**
Wayne State University, Dayton, OH
1993 - 1997
Degree: M.D.

## *Medical Training*

**Residency**
Department of Medicine
Memorial Hospital, Denver, CO
1997 - 2000
Program Director: Robert Jackson, M.D.

## *Medical Training (continued)*

- 650-bed tertiary care facility.
- Worked in inpatient and ambulatory medicine including extensive ICU, CCU, oncology, and emergency room experience.
- Performed multiple procedures including central line placement, lumbar puncture, bone marrow biopsy, and ventilator management.

**Fellow**
Neonatal Intensive Care Unit
Henry Wilkins Hospital, Cincinnati, OH
2000 - present
Program Director: James Minor, M.D.

- Comprehensive program encompassing all phases of neonatal care including Intensive Care Unit, Step-Down Unit, and Well-Baby Nurseries.
- Expect to have performed approximately 221 cranial ultrasounds, 29 EEGs, and 156 umbilical catheter placements upon completion.

## *Business Experience*

General Motors Company, Casting Division
Dearborn, MI
Financial and Profits Analysis
June 1991 - July 1993

General Motors Company, Casting Plant
Indianapolis, IN
Accounting and Financial Analysis
August 1987 - May 1991

## *Certifications*

- American Board of Internal Medicine, 1995
- Basic Cardiac Life Support Certification, 1996
- Advanced Cardiac Life Support Certification, 1996

## Professional Societies

- American Medical Association
- American College of Physicians
- American Pediatric Society
- American Academy of Pediatrics

## Licensure

State of Ohio, 2000
State of Colorado, 1999

## References

Furnished upon request.

# ALEXANDER CLARKE

85 Starview Lane • Kalamazoo, MI 49002
Home: (616) 555-6812 • Cellular: (616) 555-3448

## CAREER OBJECTIVE

*Position as a health care administrator in a hospital or clinic serving the mentally handicapped.*

## EDUCATION

Bachelor of Science, June 1995
Psychology Major, Accounting Minor
Ball State University, Muncie, Indiana

- 3.49 G.P.A.
- Kappa Delta Tau (Honor Society in Psychology)
- Dean's List (5 times)

## PROFESSIONAL EXPERIENCE

**Managing Director, Craig L. Turner Clinic**
January 2002 – present
*Responsible for all aspects of clinic operation including financial planning, personnel, and cost control. Also, coordinate all nursing and medical activities.*

**Assistant Director, Kelly Hospital**
June 1999 – December 2001
*Managed medical record department, inpatient admittance, and budget planning.*

**Administrative Supervisor, Muncie Community Hospitals**
July 1995 – May 1999
*Trained personnel, hired staff, and administered educational services.*

*References Available*

# GRAHAM T. BOOKER

2354 Fuller Place, Apt. 2C
Indianapolis, IN 46250
Home: 317-555-7896
E-mail: graham.booker@xxx.com

- *SAFETY INSTRUCTION*
- *ENVIRONMENTAL ASSESSMENT*
- *SAFETY MANAGEMENT*

## EDUCATION

Bachelor of Science, Health and Safety Education, 1997
Indiana State University, Terre Haute, Indiana

Relevant Courses:    Personal Health Science
                     Individual Safety
                     Community Health
                     Health Biostatistics
                     Health and Safety Education
                     Sociology
                     Human Anatomy
                     Human Ecology
                     Health Services
                     Epidemiology

## EXPERIENCE

**Indiana Army National Guard, Shelbyville, Indiana**
**1995 - present**

*Company Executive Officer*
1997- 2000
- Coordinated command service support requirements.
- Responsible for all logistics.
- Counseled and performed annual evaluations for personnel.
- Solicited suggestions for procedural improvements.
- Conducted all physical fitness training.
- Appointed as company Safety Officer—planned and conducted safety classes.
- Representative in the Indiana National Guard Safety Council.
- Appointed Unit Marshal—enforced military justice at the company level.

*Page 1 of 2*

**Lifeguard**
**Indiana State University Department of Recreation, Terre Haute, Indiana**
**1995 - 1997**
- Oversaw the safety of all individuals in the pool area.
- Improved and implemented safety procedures.
- Trained new lifeguards.
- Completed cardiopulmonary resuscitation and emergency first aid course.

**Distribution Services Clerk**
**AGA Fleet Products, Indianapolis, Indiana**
**1995 - 1997**
- Filled all orders.
- Coordinated all departments and their needs.
- Provided support to the company president.
- Developed and maintained databases.

## MILITARY SERVICE

- Completed Army helicopter flight school training, November 2000.
- Served as $1^{st}$ Lieutenant in the Indiana National Guard.
- Received Air Crewman's Badge, Army Service Ribbon, and the Army Commendation Medal.
- Completed Officer Candidate School while a full-time college student.

*CURRICULUM VITAE*                      THOMAS K. BODLE

555 Still Drive • Saskatoon, Saskatchewan • Canada S7J 4M7
Home: 232-555-4554 • Work: 343-555-7680
E-mail: Tbodle@xxx.com

## *EXAMINATIONS PASSED*

- FMGEMS Part I - January 1998
- Medical Council of Canada Evaluation Exam - March 1999
- FMGEMS Part II - May 1999
- Medical Council of Canada Qualifying Exam (LMCC) - May 2000
- FLEX Examination - June 2000
- FRCP (Internal Medicine, Written Component) - May 2001

## *CURRENT POSITION*

Resident IV in Internal Medicine
Department of Medicine, The Queens Hospital
Saskatoon, Saskatchewan, Canada S7N 5M8
July 2002 to present

## *EXAMINATION TAKEN AND RESULTS AWAITED*

American Board of Internal Medicine
September 24 & 25, 2002

## *ACADEMIC QUALIFICATIONS*

M.B.B.S., Indiana University, January 1987

M.D., Indiana University, September 1991
Postgraduate Specialty: Internal Medicine

Diploma, National Board of Medical Examinations, November 1994
Specialty: Nephrology

## EXPERIENCE

March 1987 - February 1988
Compulsory rotation internship in combined hospitals affiliated with Indiana Medical College in Indianapolis. Rotations included internal medicine, surgery, obstetrics and gynecology, community medicine and public health, orthopedics, psychiatry, otorhino-laryngology, ophthalmology, dermatology, and emergency medicine.

March 1988 - May 1988
Family Practice
Troy, PA

June 1988 - August 1988
Senior House Officer in Internal Medicine
Department of Medicine, Troy Medical College
Troy, PA

January 1992 - January 1994
Two years of subspecialty training as a fellow in Nephrology
Department of Nephrology, Christian Medical College & Hospital
Boston, MA

February 1994 - November 1994
Senior Registrar in Nephrology
Department of Nephrology, Christian Medical College & Hospital
Boston, MA

August 1995 - June 1997
Assistant Professor in Medicine
Department of Medicine, St. Mary's College & Hospital
Lafayette, IN

July 1997 - June 1999
Two years of fellowship training in Nephrology, Division of Nephrology
Department of Internal Medicine, University of Queens Hospital
Alberta, Canada

## EXPERIENCE (CONTINUED)

July 1999 - June 2002
Three years of core training in Internal Medicine
Department of Medicine, University of Queens Hospital
Alberta, Canada

## AWARDS AND SCHOLARSHIPS

Resident research project won top prize for 2000–2001
*Cyclosporin and Distal Renal Tubular Dysfunction in Renal Transplant Patients*
Department of Medicine, University of Queens Hospital
Alberta, Canada

Social and Educational Scholarship of the Provincial Government. Awarded for five years, 1982-1986, while attending Indiana University.

## ADMINISTRATIVE POSTS

Administrative Resident, 2000
Department of Medicine, Valley Health Center
Alberta, Canada

Organizing Secretary, October 1996
Sixth Annual Conference of the Southern Chapter of Nephrology

Coordinator, 1995
Scientific Session, Fifteenth Annual Conference of Nephrology

## PROFESSIONAL EXPERIENCE

- Investigation, diagnosis, and management of all varieties of clinical nephrology problems.
- Hemodialysis (insertion of subclavian, jugular, femoral lines; creation of Scribner shunts; monitoring; and follow-up of patients on acute and chronic peritoneal dialysis).
- Peritoneal dialysis (insertion of acute peritoneal dialysis, monitoring, and follow-up of patients on acute and chronic peritoneal dialysis).
- Renal biopsies (300 adult biopsies, 75 transplant biopsies, and 30 pediatric biopsies).
- Live donor kidney perfusion (150 kidney perfusions).
- Renal transplant recipient monitoring and post-transplant follow-up including evaluation of complications and management of rejection episodes (approximately 300 renal transplants).

## TEACHING EXPERIENCE

- Theory classes in Internal Medicine and Nephrology for undergraduate students.
- Bedside clinical teaching for undergraduate and postgraduate students in Internal Medicine.
- Seminars, grand rounds, teaching rounds, journal club meetings.
- Classes for M.S. (nursing course) in Medicine.
- Classes for dialysis diploma students.

## RESEARCH EXPERIENCE

I am interested in transplant immunology research and have completed one year of bench research studying the significance of anti-HLA Class I antibodies in renal transplant recipients and their role in the causation of rejection episodes. This work was supported by a grant from the Alberta Heritage Fund and was presented at the American Transplant Society annual meeting, held in Chicago in 1999, and the American Society of Nephrology meeting, held in Austin in 2000.

## MEMBERSHIPS

Association of Physicians of America
Southern Chapter, Society of Nephrology
Medical Association of Canada

# Omar J. Jaksa

**642 Brady Road • Westfield, NJ 07901 • Omar.Jaksa@xxx.com • 451-555-2886**

## Education

University of Texas at Austin
Degree: B.S. in Biology, 1993

URWAR Medical School, Santa Anna, D.R.
Degree: M.D., 1996

## Postgraduate Training

Transitional Internship, July 1996 - June 1997
Frankford Hospital, Troy, PA

Residency, July 1997 - June 2000
Presbyterian University of PA, Troy, PA

Nephrology Fellowship, June 2000 - present
Mt. Sinai Medical Center, New York, NY

## Examinations & Licensures

- FMGMS passed in July 1995 (ECFMG License #55555555)
- FLEX passed in June 1996
- Internal Medicine Board passed in August 2000
- DEA License #MD-55555-L in April 1998
- PA State License #555555 in April 2000
- Internal Medicine License #555555

## Memberships

- Alpha Epsilon Delta
- American College of Physicians
- American Medical Association
- Renal Physicians Association
- The National Kidney Foundation

## Background

- Volunteer Nurse's Aide in Austin, 1990
- Volunteer Physician Assistant in Austin, October 1995 - August 1996
- Fluent in English, Spanish, French, and Arabic

**JOHANNA BROWN**  133 Lincoln Drive
Detroit, MI 48099
Home: (613) 555-3361
E-mail: johanna.brown@xxx.com

## POSITION DESIRED

Health Care Administrator in a hospital or clinic.

## EXPERIENCE

**Director, Vicksburg Community Hospitals**
**1991 to present**
Responsible for all aspects of hospital operation, including financial planning, personnel, medical activities, and facilities management.

**Assistant Director, Vicksburg Community Hospitals**
**1990 to 1991**
Handled inpatient and outpatient admittance, cost control, and emergency services.

**Assistant Director, Plainwell Community Hospitals**
**1987 to 1990**
Managed billing practices, cost control, and new cost procedures.

## EDUCATION

Western Michigan University, Kalamazoo, Michigan
M.S., Public Health Administration, May 1991
B.S., Business with Biology minor, May 1987

Participated in professional in-service seminars on fiscal and health care issues: cost control, financial planning, billing and collection systems, inpatient admittance, and Lynn Hall's lecture series relating occupational therapy to the hospital environment.

## COMMUNITY SERVICE

Volunteer Firefighter in Vicksburg for 8 years. Member of the committee to study emergency care facilities in Vicksburg.

Member of the American Public Health Association and the American Academy of Hospital Administrators.

## REFERENCES

Available upon request

# ANNETTE KEITH

555 Leavitt Drive, Apt. 2 • Yonkers, NY 10710
Annette.Keith@xxx.com • (914) 555-6892

## PROFESSIONAL EXPERIENCE

July 2002 to June 2003
Fellowship in Gynecology at Albert College of Medicine, Bronx, New York

July 1999 to June 2002
Residency in Internal Medicine at New York Hospital, Queens, New York
Affiliated with New York Hospital, Cornell University, Ithaca, New York

May 1995 to October 1998
Medical Officer, Brazil, South America

October 1993 to April 1995
Postgraduate Resident at Kayo Medical College Hospital, Kayo, Mexico

April 1992 to April 1993
Rotating Internship at the Queens Hospital, Queens Medical College, and Queens
University, Bronx, New York

## CERTIFYING EXAMINATIONS

- Eligible to appear for The American Board of Obstetrics and Gynecology
  Examination, June 2003
- Diplomate of The American Board of Internal Medicine, September 2002
- FLEX, New York State (83% & 86%), December 1999
- FMGEMS (85%), January 1998

## EDUCATION

September 1987 to August 1993
Bachelor of Medicine and Bachelor of Surgery (M.B.B.S.)
Queens Medical College, Bronx, New York

June 1985 to March 1987
Premedical course at The National College
Queens University, Bronx, New York

## LICENSES
New York State, #555555
July 2002

Mexico, #5555
May 1993

## AWARDS AND HONORS
Medical
Class of 110 students
- 1st rank in first M.B.B.S. Exam
- 1st rank in second M.B.B.S. Exam
- 12th rank in final M.B.B.S. Exam

Premedical
State level examination
- 4th rank in first year
- 11th rank in second year

## MEMBERSHIPS
Member of the American College of Physicians

## REFERENCES
Dr. Sam Joseph, M.D.
Chief, Division of Obstetrics and Gynecology, Queens Medical College
Bronx, New York 10451
Phone: (718) 555-4927

Dr. Jason Wilcox, M.D.
Chief, Division of Obstetrics and Gynecology, Memorial Medical Center
Bronx, New York 10453
Phone: (718) 555-6890

Dr. Kerry Piller, M.D.
Chief, Department of Medicine, St. Joseph Medical Center
Bronx, New York 10455
Phone: (718) 555-9900

*Curriculum Vitae*

## RICHARD A. LAGNER, M.D.
### 5677 N. Senate Avenue, Suite 561
### Indianapolis, IN 64202

---

## PERSONAL DATA

Address:                          1111 N. Illinois
                                  Indianapolis, IN 46208

Telephone:                        (317) 555-3354

Pager:                            (317) 555-8891

E-mail:                           Dick.Lagner@xxx.com

Military Service:                 United States Navy
                                  Rank: Commander
                                  June 1985–July 1996

## EDUCATION AND TRAINING

Premedical:                       Notre Dame University
                                  South Bend, Indiana
                                  B.A. Degree
                                  1979–1981

Medical School:                   Indiana University
                                  Indianapolis, Indiana
                                  M.D. Degree
                                  1982–1985

Internship:                       National Naval Medical Center
                                  Bethesda, Maryland
                                  Surgical Internship
                                  1985–1986

Residency:                        Naval Regional Medical Center
                                  Portsmouth, Virginia
                                  General Surgery
                                  1986–1990

Residency continued:                    National Naval Medical Center
                                         Bethesda, Maryland
                                         Plastic Surgery
                                         1990–1992

Board Certification:                     American Board of Plastics and
                                         Reconstructive Surgery, 2000

## TEACHING POSITIONS

October 1998                             Assistant Clinical Professor
                                         Naval Regional Medical Center
                                         Microvascular Surgery Techniques

March 1999                               Memorial Medical Center
                                         Long Beach, California
                                         Hyperbaric Oxygen Therapy

May 2001                                 Midwestern Regional Lipoplasty
                                           Symposium
                                         Minneapolis, Minnesota
                                         Liposuction

## MEMBERSHIPS

International Microsurgical Society
American Burn Association
American Association of Tissue Banks
American Medical Association
Diplomate, American Board of Plastic Surgery

## DIRECTORSHIPS/CHAIRMANSHIPS

Consultant, Hyperbaric Oxygen Therapy, Memorial Medical Center, 2000–present
Chair, Decubitus Ulcer Task Force, Memorial Medical Center, 2001–present
Consultant, Tissue Bank, Central Indiana Blood Center, 2000–2001
Director, Wound Care Task Force, Memorial Medical Center, 2001–present
Burn Director, Memorial Medical Center, 2001–present

## PUBLICATIONS

"Malignant Hypothermia During Repair of a Cleft Lip," L. P. Gisler, D. Wroblewski, R. A. Lagner, *Annals of Plastic Surgery*, Vol. 2, No. 5, pp. 550–562

## PRESENTATIONS

| | |
|---|---|
| May 2001 | Clinitron Benefits<br>Guest Speaker at Support Systems International<br>St. Petersburg, Florida |
| October 2001 | Techniques of Wound Repair<br>Guest Speaker at 8th Annual Emergency Medicine Update Meeting, Community Hospital of Minneapolis |

## MEETINGS ATTENDED

| | |
|---|---|
| January 1995 | Symposia of Military Plastic Surgery<br>Washington, D.C. |
| October 1995 | American Society of Plastic and Reconstructive Surgery<br>New Orleans, Louisiana |
| October 1996 | American Association of Hand Surgery<br>New York, New York |
| April 1997 | American Burn Association Meeting<br>Cincinnati, Ohio |
| May 2000 | American Cleft Palate Association<br>Indianapolis, Indiana |
| March 2001 | Plastic Surgery Education Foundation Meeting<br>Steamboat Springs, Colorado |
| May 2002 | The Midwestern Regional Lipoplasty Symposium<br>Indianapolis, Indiana |

# EVELYN MOORE

**4366 SOUTH STREET**

**DETROIT, MI 48062**

**PHONE: (616) 555-9698**

**E-MAIL: EVE.MOORE@XXX.COM**

## CAREER GOAL

To obtain a position teaching dental hygiene

## EDUCATION

Temple University, Philadelphia, PA
M.S. Dental Hygiene, 2000

Western Michigan University, Kalamazoo, MI
B.S. Dental Hygiene, June 1998

## WORK EXPERIENCE

**Instructor of Dental Hygiene, June 2000 - present**
Western Michigan University, Kalamazoo, MI
Classes: oral anatomy, periodontology and physiology

**Graduate Assistant, September 1998 - May 2000**
Western Michigan University, Kalamazoo, MI
Duties: teaching section in periodontology and physiology, grading
assignments and quizzes, and recording attendance for lecture periods

## REFERENCES

Available upon request

# DARREN C. HANOVER

405 D Lane, Apt. 3C                          Work: (317) 555-0987
Indianapolis, IN 46237                       Home: (317) 555-8907
E-mail: Dhanover@xxx.com


## POSITION SOUGHT                           Pediatric Nurse Practitioner


## EDUCATION

**Pediatric Nurse Practitioner**
Indiana State University School of Nursing - Terre Haute, IN
Certificate as Pediatric Nurse Practitioner, 1996

Department of Postgraduate Medicine & Health Professional Education
University of Michigan Medical School - Ann Arbor, MI
Pediatric Emergency Nursing, 2000

7th Annual Nursing Conference on Pediatric Primary Care
National Association of Pediatric Nurse Associates and Practitioners -
San Diego, CA
The PNP in the Changing Health Care System, 2001

**Graduate**
Indiana State University School of Nursing - Terre Haute, IN
Master of Science in Nursing, 1995

**Undergraduate**
Medical College of Georgia - Augusta, GA
Bachelor of Science in Nursing, 1991

**Other**
Auburn Community College - Auburn, NY
Affiliation with Basic Nursing School
Taking sciences appropriate to nursing, 1987


## PROFESSIONAL CREDENTIALS

**RN License**
Indiana: #55555555 Exp. 10/31/2003
New York: #55555555 Exp. 10/31/2004

*Page 1 of 3*

**Pediatric Nurse Practitioner**
Certificate, Indiana State University School of Nursing
The National Board of Pediatric Nurse Practitioners and Associates
Certification, 1996
Pediatric Nurse Practitioner, ID #55555555

## PROFESSIONAL EXPERIENCE

**Hawley Community Hospital Clinic - Fort Wayne, IN**
**Pediatric Nurse Practitioner**
**February 1998 to present**
Duties:
- Primary care nurse in the Pediatric and Well Baby Clinic.
- Plan and develop methods, practices, and approaches pertinent to health maintenance of pediatric patients (birth to 18 years) and their families.
- The work covers a complete range of pediatric health services including assessing status of patients, evaluating the effectiveness of care, initiating or modifying treatment. This involves counseling, teaching, coordinating services, networking with other disciplines, developing new techniques, establishing and revising criteria for care.
- Also act as clinical instructor and preceptor for graduate PNP students, RN students, and medical screening students planning and executing in-services.
- Responsible, as pediatric nursing consultant for the hospital, for planning and executing parenting classes, and serve as a member of the Community Health Education Committee.

**Ireland Community Hospital - Louisville, KY**
**Pediatric Nurse Practitioner**
**July 1996 to February 1998**
Duties:
- Same duties as Fort Wayne.
- In addition, responsible for all admission and discharge physicals on normal newborns including ordering required studies and managing specific abnormalities. Gave all newborn prenatal and postnatal classes.
- Rotated as weekend hospital nursing supervisor.
- Served on the Audit and Community Health Education Committee.

**Tripler Medical Center - Honolulu, HI**
**Clinical Head Nurse**
**July 1994 to July 1996**
Duties:

- In charge of 33-bed pediatric medical-surgical ward caring for children requiring minimal to intensive care.
- Responsible for the administration and management of nursing activities on a busy pediatric ward through maximum utilization, evaluation, education, and training of nursing personnel.
- Supervised and was responsible for 10-12 RNs and 15-20 paraprofessionals and gave care to pediatric patients.
- As a clinical head nurse, responsible for assessing, planning, directing, giving, and evaluating nursing care.
- Served as hospital nursing supervisor 1-2 weekends per month and as maternal-child supervisor as needed.

**Moncrief Community Hospital - Charlotte, SC**
**Clinical Staff and Head Nurse**
**January 1993 to July 1994**
Duties:

- First 4 months worked as staff nurse for all shifts in the nursery and pediatric ward, ending as Clinical Head Nurse.
- Responsible for introducing the role of the PNP to the Pediatric Clinic.

**Madigan Medical Center - Tacoma, WA**
**Clinical Staff Nurse**
**February 1991 to December 1992**
Duties:

- Worked as staff nurse in charge of evening shift.
- This involved care and supervision of care for medical-surgical pediatric patients up to age 18 years requiring minimal to intensive care.
- Supervised RNs and paraprofessionals.

## *PROFESSIONAL ORGANIZATIONS*

National Association of Pediatric Nurse Associates and Practitioners
1998 to present

National Association of Pediatric Nurse Associates and Practitioners
Indiana Chapter
1999 to present

*References available upon request or during interview.*

# *Stephanie Johnson*

5024 Oridna Lane
Indianapolis, Indiana 64022
Phone: (317) 555-9601
E-mail: S-Johnson@xxx.com

## *Goal*
To be a dental hygienist in a family practice.

## *Education*
Marian College – Associate Degree in Dental Hygiene, 1995
Cathedral High School - Honors Diploma, 1993

## *Employment*
**Hygienist, 1999 to present**
Robert Reynolds, D.D.S.
8629 Weber Street
Indianapolis, Indiana 46022

- Examine teeth and gums.
- Clean and polish teeth.
- Take and develop x-rays.
- Screen patients for oral cancer.
- Give fluoride treatments.
- Instruct patients in home oral health procedures.

**Dental Assistant and Hygienist, 1995 to 1999**
Amanda Lindsay, D.D.S.
4825 Ridge Road
Indianapolis, Indiana 46040

- Took and developed x-rays.
- Made preliminary impressions for study casts.
- Participated in "four-hand procedures."
- Prepared filling materials and cements.
- Took impressions.
- Kept the patients comfortable.

## *References*
Available on request.

# ANDREW JOHN BEAMS

*Local Address*
786 Zelda Street
Indianapolis, IN 46831
(317) 555-2299

*Home Address*
404 W. 16th Street
South Bend, IN 46628
(219) 555-4536

## OBJECTIVE

To obtain employment in a health care environment where I can apply my knowledge of education and exercise my analytical and interpersonal skills.

## EDUCATION

**Bachelor of Science with Honors in Education, Temple University, May 2000**
- Grade Point Average - 3.3 out of 4.0

## EXPERIENCE

**Educational Attendant, June 2000 - Present**
**Tri-West Services for Mental Health, South Bend, IN**
- Involved in one-on-one contact with patients on the unit, taking vital signs, directing recreational activities, and completing rounds.
- Responsible for charting on individual patients and providing assessments of patients' physical and mental status.

**Reformat Editor, February 1999 - May 2000**
**Valley, Inc., Indianapolis, IN**
- Member of a four-person effort to reformat Valley's All Lines Service (covering insurance agent/agency licensing) from a word processing format into a database format.

**Research Assistant, August 1998 - May 2000**
**Department of Science, Temple University, IN**
- Assisted in scoring, coding, analyzing, and interpreting data in various research areas.

**Computer Lab Assistant, August 1996 - May 2000**
**Temple University, IN**
- Assisted students with Macintosh usage.

## SPECIAL SKILLS

I have worked with Macintosh computers and Microsoft Word extensively, and I am familiar with Delta Graph, HyperCard, and Excel. Also, I have had experience with two statistical packages, Super ANOVA and SPSSx, and I become acquainted with new software packages quickly.

## ACTIVITIES

- Member of the Phi Delta Theta Fraternity
- Alumni secretary, Fall 1998
- Pledge committee member, Fall 1997
- Intramural softball
- Member of the Education Club, Spring 1999 to Present
- Peer academic advisor, Fall 1999

## REFERENCES

Available upon request

# JANE R. REYNOLDS

*1241 Rue Louis XVI*
*Montreal, Quebec 42T 3T1*
*Voice mail: 514-555-1926*
*E-mail: Jane.Reynolds@xxx.com*

## ■ SECONDARY SCHOOL / UNIVERSITY

- Concordia University, 1999 to 2003
- St. Brides' High School, 1993 to 1999

## ■ EXAMINATIONS ACHIEVED

- Certificate of SYS Chemistry, grade A, 1999
- English, Mathematics, Biology, Chemistry, grade B, 1998

GRADES IN PHARMACY B.Sc. COURSES

| | |
|---|---|
| Pharmaceutical Chemistry | 83% |
| Pharmaceutics | 57% |
| Pharmacy Practice | 74% |
| Drugs and Disease | 70% |
| Drug Disposition and Biopharmaceutics | 84% |

## ■ EMPLOYMENT

Dispenser
Summer Employment, 2001, 2002, and 2003
Robert G. Gross, M.R.Pharm.S.

## ■ REFERENCES

Available on Request

# PAULINE S. BIRCH
1610 Willow Lane • New Haven, KY 57220
(613) 555-1583 • P.Birch@xxx.com


**Position Desired:**        School Psychologist

**Education:**               North Salem University
                             B.A. Psychology, 1994

                             Bellaire University
                             M.A. Psychology, 1996

                             Williamshire University
                             Ed.S. School Psychology, 2002

**Certification:**           School Psychologist I

**Work Experience:**         June 2001 to Present
                             Williamshire University
                             Counseling and Testing Clinic
                             Position: Part-time Graduate Assistant

                             April 1998 to June 2001
                             Kramer Clinic
                             Position: Addictions Counselor

                             December 1994 to April 1996
                             Children's Services
                             Position: Counselor

                             November 1992 to December 1994
                             Comp-tek, Inc.
                             Position: Office Manager

**Memberships:**             Student Representative
                             Williamshire University Graduate
                             Council

                             Vice President
                             Association of Graduate Counselors
                             Williamshire University

## KEVIN E. CODY

5555 Field Avenue
Fort Wayne, IN 46236
Cellular: (219) 555-8976
E-mail: K.E.Cody@xxx.com

## OBJECTIVE

*Staff nurse anesthetist position with room for supervisory advancement within two years in a modern, well-equipped, mid-sized medical facility where CRNAs and MDAs support each other while retaining their own autonomy.*

## SUMMARY OF QUALIFICATIONS

Clinical experience in small and large medical center settings, combining decision making with professional latitude. Experienced in all types of general and regional anesthesia with continuous epidural experience in postoperative pain relief. Possess strong interpersonal communication skills resulting in high degrees of patient satisfaction.

## EDUCATION

Webster University, Master of Arts in Health Services Management, 2003

Baylor University, Bachelor of Science in Nursing, 1999

Academy of Health Sciences, Diploma in Nurse Anesthesia, 1996

## EXPERIENCE

**Staff Anesthetist and Chief Anesthetist, Nurse Anesthesia Section**
**2003 to present**
**Hawley Community Hospital, Fort Wayne, IN**

- Supervise and assume overall clinical and administrative responsibility for a two-anesthetist operating setting averaging over 500 cases per year without the benefit of an assigned staff anesthesiologist.

# EXPERIENCE (Continued)

- Serve as technical director and quality assurance coordinator for Respiratory Therapy Services. Perform duties of chief, Department of Nursing, in her absence.
- Administer clinical anesthesia with call coverage, and provide continuous epidural postoperative pain management.

**Staff Anesthetist and Assistant Supervisor, Nurse Anesthesia Section**
**2001 to 2003**
**Brooke Medical Center, Houston, TX**

- Provided relief supervision and assistance to CRNA staff and anesthesia residents administering anesthesia on complex surgical procedures.
- Assisted with anesthesia supplies and new equipment ordering, maintenance, and evaluation.
- Served as a Basic Cardiac Life Support (BCLS) instructor for the anesthesia staff.
- Administered clinical anesthesia in medical center and Level I trauma center setting.

**Chief and Assistant Chief, Nurse Anesthesia Section**
**1999 to 2001**
**Moncrief Community Hospital, Charlotte, SC**

- Supervised staff of four CRNAs in operative setting averaging over 200 surgical cases per month.
- Managed anesthesia supply system resulting in successful compliance with projected budgetary constraints.
- Converted daily anesthesia supply system to a daily cart exchange system to reduce time spent on daily restock.
- Administered clinical anesthesia with call coverage.

**Staff Anesthetist and Clinical Instructor, Nurse Anesthesia Section**
**1998 to 1999**
**Community Hospital, Richmond, VA**

- Provided clinical supervision of Community Hospital, Phase II nurse anesthesia students.
- Designed a departmental continuing education program with approved credit by the American Association of Nurse Anesthetists (AANA). Developed a departmental quality assurance program.
- Administered clinical anesthesia with call coverage.

## EXPERIENCE (Continued)

**Staff Anesthetist, Nurse Anesthesia Section**
**1996 to 1998**
**Memorial Hospital, Tulsa, OK**

- Developed departmental quality assurance program.
- Developed departmental continuing education program with approved credit by the AANA.
- Developed a standardized anesthesia equipment setup for hospital-wide use in all CPR carts.
- Evaluated and gained approval for purchase of a new anesthesia gas mass spectrometry monitoring system.
- Administered clinical anesthesia with call coverage.

## AFFILIATIONS

American Association of Nurse Anesthetists, member since 1996

## LICENSURE

Board of Nursing Examiners for the State of Texas No. 55555555

Indiana State Board of Nursing No. 5555 (temporary permit)

## CERTIFICATION

Council on Recertification of Nurse Anesthetists No. 55555

# David Edward Garcia

17644 Ventura Blvd. • Los Angeles, CA 90024
Phone: (213) 555-9876 • Pager: (213) 555-0036

• Registered medical laboratory technician

• Fluent in English and Spanish

## EDUCATION

A.A., Riverside Junior College
Riverside, CA, 1996

## EMPLOYMENT

Southern California Laboratories, Los Angeles, CA
August 2002 - Present
Medical Laboratory Technician

U.C.L.A. Outpatient Clinic, Los Angeles, CA
June 2001 - July 2002
Medical Laboratory Technician

Lowell Pharmaceuticals, Riverside, CA
May 1996 - May 2001
Medical Laboratory Technician

## MEMBERSHIPS

Internal Society for Clinical Laboratory Technology

## REFERENCES

Available on Request

# Samuel Ho

*9845 Corning Drive • Denver, CO 80233*
*(303) 555-9347 • Samuel.Ho@xxx.com*

## Objective

A position as ombudsman in a large teaching hospital

## Education

Boston University, Boston, Massachusetts
M.S., Health Advocacy, 1999

Saint John's College, Annapolis, Maryland
B.A., Psychology, 1994

## Experience

**Boston HMO, Boston, Massachusetts, June 2000 – Present**
Individualize health care for patients and conduct sensitivity training
sessions for staff members.

**St. John's Hospital, Annapolis, Maryland, June 1996 – June 2000**
Resolved problems of individual patients, especially the elderly, and secured
appropriate post-hospitalization services for patients.

**Cambridge Nursing Center, Cambridge, Massachusetts
May 1994 – June 1996**
Acted on behalf of indigent patients.

## Additional Information

Computer Skills: Microsoft Office Suite 2000, Lotus 1-2-3

Foreign Language: Chinese

## Affiliations

American Psychology Association

National Society for Patient Representation and Consumer Affairs of the
American Hospital Association

# Patrick R. Collen

876 West 9th Street  •  Crawfordsville, IN 47331
Pat.Collen@xxx.com  •  (317) 555-9240

## Objective

To gain a position in nutritional care.

## Education

M.S. in Nutrition, 1999
Wabash College, Crawfordsville, IN

B.S. in Dietetics, 1993
Wabash College, Crawfordsville, IN

## Experience

8/2002 to Present
Dietary Director, Wabash Hospital, Wabash, IN
Supervise in-depth nutritional assessment of patients on hyperalimentation. Supervise educational programs on weight reduction, diabetes, and geriatric nutrition.

5/1999 to 8/2002
Consultant Dietitian (part-time), Veterans Hospital, Indianapolis, IN
Developed standards for nutritional care.

4/1993 to 4/1999
Clinical Dietitian, St. Mary's Hospital, South Bend, IN
Created cost-effective nourishment center. Established nutritional care standards for individuals with HIV virus for use by local dietitians.

## Skills

- Fluent in German, proficient in French
- Skilled in use of WordPerfect and ClarisWorks
- Excellent verbal communication skills
- Experienced public speaker

*References available upon request*

# ALICIA ALVAREZ

**9867 ASHTON ROAD     LEXINGTON, KY 40506**
**A.ALVAREZ@XXX.COM                (606) 555-3494**

## OBJECTIVE

*To obtain a position as a respiratory therapist with a hospital interested in using my skills as a technical resource person. Prefer to move into management as department director.*

## EDUCATION

Bachelors Degree in Respiratory Therapy
Louisiana Tech Institute - Ruston, LA
June 2000

## EXPERIENCE

**Respiratory Therapist**
**Lexington General Hospital, Lexington, KY**
April 2002 - present
- Supervised staff respiratory technicians.
- Served as resource person for hospital staff.

**Respiratory Therapist**
**Kentucky Clinic, Lexington, KY**
August 2000 - March 2002
- Participated in the diagnosis, evaluation, and prevention of respiratory problems.

## ADDITIONAL CREDENTIALS

- Registered Respiratory Therapist
- Member, American Academy of Respiratory Therapists

## REFERENCES

*Personal and professional references on request.*

# ◆ MARY ELLEN BOYD

65 Maple Drive • Carmel, IN 46032

(317) 555-9843 • Mary.Boyd@xxx.com

## OBJECTIVE

To obtain a position as a respiratory therapist utilizing my experience in the long-term treatment of geriatric patients.

## EDUCATION

Medford Technical School, Medford, MA
March 2001

## COURSE WORK

- ◆ Biology, Chemistry, Physics
- ◆ Physiology
- ◆ Airway Management, Pharmacology
- ◆ Gas, Aerosol, and Humidity Therapy
- ◆ Pulmonary Rehabilitation
- ◆ Cardiopulmonary Anatomy
- ◆ Stress Analysis
- ◆ Software Engineering
- ◆ Mechanical Ventilation
- ◆ Ethics of Respiratory Therapy
- ◆ Systems and Disorders of Breathing

## EXPERIENCE

Respiratory Therapist
March 2001 - Present
Humana Hospital, Medford, MA

- ◆ Perform tests to evaluate and diagnose respiratory problems.
- ◆ Develop preoperative visitation program for surgical patients.
- ◆ Instruct patients in the use of respiratory treatment aids and methods.

## REFERENCES

Available on request

*Curriculum Vitae*

# Michael Martinez

455 Lilac Lane • Mooresville, IN 46158 • Martinez1@xxx.com • 317-555-7892

## EDUCATION

B.A. from Hanover College, Hanover, Indiana, 1999
• Magna Cum Laude, 3.93 G.P.A.
• Highest Departmental Honors in Chemistry, 4.0 G.P.A.
• All-American Football Lineman, Co-Captain in Senior Year
• Four Varsity Letters
• National Football Foundation and Hall of Fame Scholar Athlete Award

M.D. from Indiana University School of Medicine, Indianapolis, Indiana, 2003
• Honors Marks: Gross Anatomy and Systemic Pathology
• Clerkships in Pediatrics and Neuroscience

## MILITARY EXPERIENCE

Second Lieutenant Medical Officer Training, 2000-2003
Corps - United States Army Reserve, Indiana National Guard

Indiana Medical Advisory Committee Member, 2002

## WORK EXPERIENCE

Extern, Henry County Memorial Hospital, New Castle, Indiana, 2001-2002
Summer Research Intern, Methodist Sports Clinic, Indianapolis, Indiana, 2001

## RESEARCH EXPERIENCE

Senior Research Thesis in Department of Chemistry, Hanover College, 1998-1999
Robert M. Gibbons, Ph.D.
Associate Professor of Chemistry, Hanover, Indiana

Summer Research at St. Vincent's Sports Clinic, Indianapolis, Indiana, 1998
Andrew M. Sporn, M.D.
Director of Research and Development

## PUBLICATIONS

1. Gibbons R. M., and M. Martinez: "Forward and Reverse Rate Constants in the Diel-Alder Reaction." Senior Research Thesis File, Duggan Library, Hanover College, Hanover, Indiana, May 1999.

2. Sporn, A., M. Jones, M. Martinez, and K. L. Jones: "Isolated Fractures of the Tibial Eminence in Adults Associated with Anterior Laxity." *Journal of Sports Medicine*, Spring 2002.

## MEDICAL ILLUSTRATIONS

1. Kingsman, M. A.: "Neurovascular Injuries in the Wrists and Hands of Athletes," *Clinics in Sports Medicine*, Vol. 9, No. 2, April 2001.

2. Michaels, J. B., and M. E. Tory: "Meniscal Transplantation," Presentation, Duke University School of Medicine, Durham, North Carolina, May 2002.

# Paula Thomas

974 Chestnut Hill Road • Newark, DE 19713
Paula_Thomas@xxx.com • (302) 555-9812

---

## Qualifications

Ten years' experience in medical social work in a hospital
environment as a certified social worker.

---

## Education

Master's degree in Social Work
University of Delaware
Newark, Delaware, 2002

Bachelor's degree in Social Work
University of Delaware
Newark, Delaware, 2000

Honors Diploma
Newark High School
Newark, Delaware, 1996

Rotary Exchange Student - Germany, 1994

Various A.C.S.W. Seminars

---

## Work Experience

Leader of the Hospital Health Team
October 2003 to present
Atlantic Hospital
Newark, Delaware

• Coordinate the services of doctors, nurses, and other hospital health
care professionals to ensure that all resources are employed in the
recovery of individual patients.

## Work Experience (continued)

Supervisor of the Pediatric Unit
June 2003 to October 2003
Atlantic Hospital
Newark, Delaware

- Help ease fears of parents and children about patients' medical condition.
- Conduct family assessments.
- Refer parents to appropriate community services.

Community Health Services Coordinator
July 2000 to June 2003
Chocorus Community Hospital
Chocorus, New Hampshire

- Found homes for children without caretakers because of parental hospitalization.
- Helped elderly who needed nursing assistance in their own homes.
- Educated patients on health services available in community.
- Counseled patients on handling finances and family relationships changed by hospitalization.

## Affiliations

- American Association of University Women
- Girls' Club of Chocorus

## References

Available upon request

# JOHN J. ALLEN

**Present Address**
765 5th Street
Washington, D.C. 20016
(202) 555-2213

**Permanent Address**
28 Octavia Terrace
Washington, D.C. 20019
(202) 555-9737

## OBJECTIVE

Obtain a full-time position as a medical writer for a pharmaceutical company, medical school, textbook publisher, or government agency.

## EDUCATION

Currently pursuing M.S. in Technical Writing with a concentration in Biology.
Graduate: May 2003
George Washington University

B.S. with Highest Distinction in English, May 2000
Whitman College

## EXPERIENCE

**SUMMER INTERN**
Eli Lily and Company, Indianapolis, IN
Summer 2002
Analyzed new product data and prepared reports for in-house use by sales staff. Interviewed researchers and prepared articles for company publications.

**SUMMER INTERN**
*Washington Post*, Washington, D.C.
Summer 2001
Wrote columns on health fads, fitness, and new drugs.

## CREDENTIALS

- A.M.W.A. certificates in pharmaceutical writing and editing
- Member, American Medical Writers Association
- Editor, Whitman College newspaper

REFERENCES AVAILABLE ON REQUEST

# Harold K. Johnson

131 Palm Drive
Valparaiso, IN 46438
E-mail: HKJohnson@xxx.com
Phone: (219) 555-2232

## Summary

- Ten years' surgical technologist experience with a proven record of competence.
- Solid background in supporting operating room team in military hospitals.
- Excellent skills in planning and organizing operating room for a clean surgical environment.

## Education

Associate degree, Surgical Technology
Rochester Institute of Technology, Rochester, NY, 1993

## Certification

Certified Surgical Technologist

## Work Experience

Surgical Technology Supervisor, 1997-Present
United States Army
Fort Sill Army Hospital
- Responsible for coordinating efforts of medical technologist, scrub technologist, and circulating surgical technologist.
- Specialist in orthopedic procedures.

Surgical Technologist, 1993-1997
Paxton Memorial Hospital
- Responsible for checking supplies and equipment; draping the sterile field; and operating EKG monitors, lights, and suction machines.

## References

Available upon request

# ◆ LESLIE P. CHANDLER ◆

4812 Burlington Drive • Indianapolis, IN 46033 • (317) 555-1052
LPChandler@xxx.com

## ◆ OVERVIEW

- ◆ Retired from United States Marine Corps in February 1991.
- ◆ Currently employed as Certified Prosthetist, Manager, and part-time consultant.
- ◆ Experience in design, manufacturing, and service of prosthetic components.
- ◆ Assist prosthetic clinics with patient evaluation, management, and prosthetic care.

## ◆ EMPLOYMENT

Indianapolis Artificial Limb Corporation
May 1991 to Present
Manager, Prosthetic Design and Service Division

Veterans Administration Medical Center
September 1994 to Present
Management Consultant

Muncie Memorial Hospital
March 1995 to Present
Patient Management Consultant

## ◆ PROSTHETIC EDUCATION

Northwestern University, School of Prosthetics
Chicago, Illinois
Courses Studied:
- ◆ Below Knee Prosthetics for Prosthetists
- ◆ Above Knee Prosthetics for Prosthetists
- ◆ Upper Extremity Prosthetics for Prosthetists
- ◆ Review Course in Prosthetics
- ◆ Immediate Post-Surgical Fitting for Prosthetists

University of California
UCLA Extension, Los Angeles, CA
Course Studied:
- ◆ Suction Below Knee Prosthetics

*Page 1 of 2*

### ◆ PROSTHETIC CERTIFICATION

- ◆ American Board Certification: October 9, 1990
- ◆ Qualified Prosthetist: May 15, 1990 - License #555

### ◆ INDUSTRIAL TRAINING

Otto Bock Orthopedic Industry, Inc.
Minneapolis, Minnesota
Course Studied:
- ◆ Lower Extremity Modular System

Motion Control
Salt Lake City, Utah
Course Studied:
- ◆ Fitting Procedures of the Utah Artificial Arm

Durr-Fillauer Medical, Inc.
Chattanooga, Tennessee
Course Studied:
- ◆ Scandinavian Flexible Socket

IPOS
Niagara Falls, New York
Course Studied:
- ◆ Flexible Socket Fabrication

Otto Bock Orthopedic Industry, Inc.
Minneapolis, Minnesota
Course Studied:
- ◆ Myoelectrically Controlled Upper Extremity
- ◆ System MYOBOCK

Flex-Foot, Inc.
Irving, California
Course Studied:
- ◆ Basic Flex-Foot

REFERENCES AVAILABLE UPON REQUEST

# JILL NELSON

Current Address:                                          Permanent Address:
897 Burlingame Avenue                                     5311 Rosalind, Apt. #3
Atlanta, GA 30319                                         Calumet City, IL 60409
(404) 555-9112                                            (708) 555-9991

OBJECTIVE        Seeking an applied research and development of manufactur-
                 ing position in the field of health care products.

EDUCATION        M.S., Materials Science & Marketing
                 Princeton University - May 2003

                 B.S., Mechanical Engineering
                 University of California - May 2001

EXPERIENCE       Research Assistant
                 • Investigated the micromechanical as well as the macro-
                   mechancial properties of a ceramic matrix–ceramic fiber
                   composite.
                 • Prepared testing specimens, and performed various mechan-
                   ical testing schemes including three, four point bending and
                   tensile test.
                 • Progress of the research was supervised by Dr. James Worth.

                 Lab Consultant
                 • Helped students debugging programs written in FORTRAN.

                 Research Assistant
                 • Investigated the possibility of two-polymer systems being the
                   precursor of a superconducting material.
                 • Various compositions of the polymer solutions were pre-
                   pared, and fibers were spun via several methods.
                 • High temperature mechanical testings were carried out to
                   determine the survivability of the fiber under pyrolysis.

MEMBERSHIP       Student Chapter, American Society of Mechanical Engineers

REFERENCES       Available upon request

# Jeffrey Lien

*1908 Ohana Street*
*Honolulu, HI 96825*
*Jeff.Lien@xxx.com*
*(808) 555-9090*

## Education

B.S. Biomedical Engineering Technology, 2002
Purdue University, Lafayette, IN

## Experience

2002 - Present
Whitehall and Miles, Inc.
Honolulu, HI

- Member of health and research teams, applying the principles and technologies of various disciplines to the understanding, defining, and solving of medical and biological problems.
- Specialize in helping to develop the artificial lung, nuclear magnetic resonance, respiratory and cardiac pacemakers, and plastic heart valves.
- Engaged in the analysis and testing of different materials to determine whether they will be accepted or rejected when used in the body in artificial organs and grafts.

## Additional Skills

Fluent in Spanish
Working knowledge of German, French, and Italian

## References

Available upon request

# MARK JONES

*1031 116th St. • Indianapolis, IN 46202 • M.Jones@xxx.com • (780) 555-2310*

## OBJECTIVE
*To utilize my professional abilities to obtain a position in the field of nursing.*

## EDUCATION
Academy of Health Sciences, Fort Worth, TX
EMT/Medical Assistant Certificate, 1998

Gorgas Army Hospital, Fort Worth, TX
Enhanced Acute Trauma Certificate, 2000

Vincennes University, Vincennes, IN
General Studies, 34 semester hours, 2003

Lawrence Fire Department
EMT Defibulator
Indiana State Certificate, 2003

## WORK EXPERIENCE

2003 - present     U.S. Army; Fort Harrison, IN, Army Hospital
*Pediatric Clinician*

2001 - 2003     U.S. Army; Fort Harrison, IN, Army Hospital
*Nurse's Aide*

1999 - 2001     U.S. Army; Fort Harrison, IN, Army Hospital
*Medical Assistant/Phlebotomist*

1998 - 1999     U.S. Army; Fort Worth, TX, 5th/87th Infantry
*Emergency Medical Technician*

## AWARDS
Good Conduct Medal, U.S. Army - 1998 to 2001

REFERENCES AVAILABLE UPON REQUEST

# Patricia Allen, RRA

645 Green Street
Bloomington, IN 47403
(812) 555-8765
P.Allen@xxx.com

## Work History

**2003 - Present**
**St. Vincent's Hospital, Indianapolis, IN**
**Medical Records Administrator**
- Implement new system for retrieving medical records.
- Develop policies for processing insurance requests.
- Analyze patient data for processing insurance requests.
- Analyze patient data for hospital care programs.
- Supervise medical records clerks and transcriptionists.
- Develop in-service program for medical records clerks.
- Evaluate hospital medical records system.

**1999 - 2002**
**Purdue Clinic, Lafayette, IN**
**Medical Records Administrator**
- Assisted staff in evaluating efficiency of patient medical care.
- Analyzed patient health care programs.
- Supervised all medical records clerks.

## Education

**1998 - 2002**
**Purdue University, Lafayette, IN**
**Bachelor of Science in Medical Records Administration**
**Courses:** Anatomy, Medical Records Administration, Statistics, Disease Classification, Medical Law, Computer Science, Medical Terminology.

## Certification

Registered Records Administrator, 2002

# Jill MacFarland

419 Pierce Street

Lincolnwood, Illinois 60646

J.Macfarland@xxx.com

(847) 555-5739

## Objective

To obtain a position as a pharmacist in a retail drugstore.

## Education

University of Chicago
Senior Honors Student/Department of Pharmacology
Degree Expected: June 2003

## Experience

**Teaching Assistant, 8/02 to Present**
Pharmacology Department, University of Chicago
Assist professors with grading papers, basic research tasks, tutoring students.

**Part-time Cashier, 7/01 to 8/02**
Star Discount Store, Evanston, Illinois
Check-out cashier for retail store.
Developed excellent cash management and customer relations skills.
Trained new hires.

**Administrative Assistant, Summers 1999, 2000**
Stevenson Electrical, Skokie, Illinois
Assisted executives with document preparation, data entry, and general office duties.

## Community Service

Volunteer, Summer 2001
Habitat for Humanity

Volunteer Tutor, Adult Literacy Program, 2000 to 2001
Chicago Public Libraries

## References

Dr. Daniel Wright, Lecturer
University of Chicago
(312) 555-6174, ext. 912
D.Wright@xxx.com

Mr. Richard Woerner, Pharmacist
Star Discount Store
(847) 555-9167
Richard.Woerner@xxx.com

# Alan Frederick Smith, M.D.

*Associate in Medicine • Department of Nephrology*
*Co-Director of Dialysis Center, VA Hospital*

Home Address                                           Office Address
8 Dunmore Court                              Division of Nephrology, Box 3036
Durham, North Carolina 27713                  Duke University Medical Center
Alan.Smith@xxx.com                             Durham, North Carolina 27710
(919) 555-0918                                          (919) 555-5043

Degrees:                    B.S., Biomath, Union College, 1996
                            M.D., Duke University, 2002

Education:                  Duke University School of Medicine
                            Durham, North Carolina
                            Nephrology Fellowship, 2000 - 2002

Research Experience:        Duke University Medical Center, July 2002 - Present
                            Department of Nephrology
                            Joseph P. Major, M.D.
                            Conducted clinical trials and basic lab research on
                            metallic bone disease.

                            Durham VA Hospital, August 2000 - April 2002
                            Duke University Medical Center
                            Renal Physiology Laboratory
                            Department of Medicine
                            Mark George, M.D., and Carl Kline, M.D.
                            Relating products of renal arachidonic acid metab-
                            olism to mechanisms of cell injury and cell death.

Research Experience:
SUNY, Summer 1999
Department of Surgery
Richard Alden, M.D.
Five-year retrospective study of postoperative
complications and failure rate of herniorrhaphy at
SUNY Stony Brook, NY, Surgical Hernia Clinic.

Specialty:
Board Certified Internal Medicine, 2002

Licensure:
North Carolina License of Medicine, 2002

Research Support:
National Institutes of Health
Training Grant Research Award, 2001 - 2002

Honors:
- Magna Cum Laude, Union College
- AOA Symposium Poster Presentation
- Duke University Medical Center
- Assistant Chief Resident, Duke University Medical Center, April - June 2000
- Supervised the residency program at Durham Regional Hospital

References:
On request

# Monica Rodriquez

5092 Ashland Drive
Indianapolis, IN 46220
Work: (317) 555-8000
Home: (317) 555-2989
E-mail: M.Rodriquez@xxx.com

## Education

Undergraduate
Walsh College
Canton, Ohio
- Bachelor of Arts—double major in biology and chemistry, 1994

Graduate
Indiana University
College of Medicine
Indianapolis, Indiana
- Medical Doctor, 1998

Postgraduate
Indiana University Hospital
Indianapolis, Indiana
- Internal Medicine Internship, 6/88 - 6/94
- Internal Medicine Residency, 6/99 - 6/01
- Nephrology Fellowship, 6/01 - Present

## Credentials

- National Board of Medical Examiners Certificate
- State Medical License for Indiana, 1999
- American Board of Internal Medicine, 2001

## Grants

National Kidney Foundation of Indiana Affiliate, Mechanisms of Glomerular Injury: Lipid Induced Production of Monocyte Chemotactic Factor by Cultured Mesangial Cells, 2001 - 2002

## Academic Honors and Awards

Valedictorian Walsh College, G.P.A. 4.0
Walsh College Academic Scholarship
Three Walsh College Honors Certificates

Outstanding Junior Chemist from Walsh College in Akron section of the American Chemical Society

Letter of Commendation in Internal Medicine
Letter of Honors in Family Medicine

Veterans Association Award for Outstanding Performance at the Veterans Clinic in Indianapolis, Indiana

## Associations

- American Medical Association
- Indiana Medical Association

## Research

Compiled drug elution timetables with capillary gas chromatographs at Accutox Toxicology Laboratory, 1993 - 1994.

**REFERENCES AVAILABLE**

# • Peter Joseph Little •

354 Long Hill Road • Middletown, CT 06457 • (203) 555-9998
Peter.Little@xxx.com

## • <u>OBJECTIVE</u>

Seeking a rewarding and challenging position in medical record administration where I can utilize over ten years of experience in the medical
information field.

## • <u>CAREER SUMMARY</u>

**MEDICAL RECORD TECHNICIAN, December 2000 - Present**
JOHNSON MEMORIAL HOSPITAL
Middletown, CT 06457

- Started introductory steps in replacing existing PC hardware in client
  base.
- Directed initial stages of development on new software module for
  insurance companies.
- Provided direction to all medical record clerks and medical record
  transcriptionists.

**MEDICAL RECORD TECHNICIAN, January 1996 - November 2000**
DELTA COMMUNITY HOSPITAL
Indianapolis, IN 46280

- Responsible for analyzing records, cross-indexing medical information,
  and reviewing.
- Designed and implemented disease coding system.

**MEDICAL RECORD CLERK, August 1992 - November 1995**
COMMUNITY NORTH HOSPITAL
Indianapolis, IN 46240

- Entered codes in patients' records, maintained registries, and gathered
  statistics on studies of bed utilization and operating room usage.

## • <u>EDUCATION</u>

NATIONAL TECHNOLOGY INSTITUTE
Rochester, NY
Associate Degree, 1992
Medical Record Technician

REFERENCES AVAILABLE

# MARY ELLEN WHITE

**School Address**
Duke University
P.O. Box 55
Durham, NC 27706
(919) 555-9087

**Home Address**
345 Prospect Road
Cleveland, OH 44136
Mary.White@xxx.com
(419) 555-9087

## CAREER OBJECTIVE

A position in biomedical engineering with emphasis on developing artificial organs and joints.

## EDUCATION

Master of Science, Duke University
May 2002

Bachelor of Science, Duke University
May 2000

## WORK EXPERIENCE

**United Technologies**
Edinburgh, IN
May 2001 to September 2001
- Tested artificial joint materials.
- Studied therapeutic devices.

**Duke University Biomedical Laboratory**
Durham, NC
August 2000 to May 2001
- Participated in labs analyzing synthetic organ tissues.
- Developed new strategies for producing synthetic materials.

## HONORS AND ACTIVITIES

- Society of Women Engineers
- Phi Sigma Tau engineering sorority
- American Society of Biomedical Engineers

REFERENCES AVAILABLE

# JANE P. WHITLOCK

5 Maple Street
South Bend, IN 46237
(219) 555-7892
Jane.Whitlock@xxx.com

## JOB OBJECTIVE

*To acquire a clinical position in a physical therapy facility emphasizing orthopedics and sports medicine, while continuing to develop my interest in occupational therapy.*

## EXPERIENCE

Memorial Hospital, 6/02 - present
634-bed acute care facility
- Staff therapist, responsible for managing outpatient department.
- Worked closely with a neurosurgeon in developing an exercise program for post-op patients.

Nappanee Hospital, 3/98 - 6/02
254-bed acute care facility
- Responsible for inpatient and outpatient physical therapy care with participation in a sports medicine clinic.
- Handled burn and multiple-trauma patients.

## EDUCATION

University of Ohio, Bachelor of Science in Physical Therapy, 1998

## PROFESSIONAL ORGANIZATIONS

Member, American Physical Therapy Association

## REFERENCES

*Available upon request*

# Curriculum Vitae

Gordon A. Rosin
Major, United States Army
5711 Norman Ave.
Ft. Worth, TX 76103

**Present Position**

Assistant Chief Nurse Anesthetist
Bradley Army Community Hospital
Ft. Worth, TX

**Educational Background**

Troy State University
Troy, AL
B.S.N. 1990

Texas Wesleyan University
Fort Worth, TX
M.S. 1997

**Military Schools and Courses**

Clinical Specialist Course 91C
Army Medical Department
William Beaumont Army Medical Center
El Paso, TX
1992

Medical Field Service School
Academy of Health Sciences
Fort Sam Houston, TX
1993

AMEDD Officers Advanced Course E-23
Academy of Health Sciences
Fort Sam Houston, TX
1995

Combined Officers Advanced Staff
  Services School
Fort Leavenworth, KS
1996

MILITARY SCHOOLS
AND COURSES
(CONTINUED)

School of Anesthesiology for Army Nurse
  Corps Officers, Phase I
Academy of Health Sciences
Fort Sam Houston, TX
1997

School of Anesthesiology for Army
  Nurse Corps Officers, Phase II
Academy of Health Sciences
Darnell Army Community Hospital
Fort Hood, TX
1998

AMEDD Officers Clinical Head Nurse
  Course
Academy of Health Sciences
Fort Sam Houston, TX
1998

LICENSES

- Registered Nurse, Alabama, 1990,
  #5-55555
- Registered Nurse, Texas, 1997, #555555
- Certified Registered Nurse Anesthetist,
  TX 1999, #5555
- Registered Nurse, Indiana, 2001,
  #55555555

PROFESSIONAL
SOCIETIES

American Association of Nurse Anesthetists, 2000

UNITED STATES
ARMY SERVICE

Assistant Chief Nurse Anesthetist
Bradley Army Community Hospital
Fort Worth, TX
2001 - present

Staff Nurse Anesthetist
William Beaumont Army Medical Center
El Paso, TX
1999 - 2001

CIVILIAN
EXPERIENCE

Obstetric Anesthesia, Part-time
Vista Hills Medical Center
El Paso, TX
1998 - 2001

Obstetric Anesthesia, Part-time
Sierra Medical Center
El Paso, TX
1995 - 1998

Staff Nurse, Ortho/ICU, Part-time
Jackson Hospital
Montgomery, AL
1992 - 1995

## SUSAN MARIE COOPER

111 Central Avenue • Indianapolis, IN 46268
Home: (317) 555-9087 • Cellular: (317) 555-6477

## EMPLOYMENT

Staff Occupational Therapist, Registered
3/02 - Present
Occupational Therapy Department
Indiana Hand Center
Indianapolis, IN 46237

Staff Occupational Therapist
1/99 - 3/02
Occupational Therapy Department
St. Joseph Medical Center
South Bend, IN 46637

Occupational Therapy Assistant
1/96 - 1/99
Occupational Therapy Department
Elkhart Memorial Hospital
Elkhart, IN 46417

## EDUCATION

Indiana University, 1996
Bachelor of Science
Occupational Therapy

## SPECIAL PROJECTS

Private Practice: Pediatrics, Independent Study

## AFFILIATIONS

• American Occupational Therapy Association
• Indiana Occupational Therapy Association

## REFERENCES

Available Upon Request

# DONNA A. POWELL

555 W. Scott Street • Indianapolis, IN 46628
D.Powell@xxx.com
Home: (317) 555-8972 • Pager: (317) 555-0988

## JOB OBJECTIVE

To work in a neonatal nursery as a clinical specialist involved
in the support of infants and children.

## EDUCATION

Bachelor of Science in Nursing, 2000
Purdue University - Lafayette, IN
Graduated with honors

## EXPERIENCE

Wishard Hospital, Indianapolis, IN
June 2000 to Present
Staff nurse in the neonatal intensive care unit.

## AFFILIATIONS

Indiana Nurses Association
National Association of Neonatal Nurses

## REFERENCES

On request

# PAM T. PHILLIPS

444 Mulberry Street
Carmel, IN 46032
(317) 555-7624
pamela.phillips@xxx.com

## JOB OBJECTIVE

To work in a neonatal nursery as a specialist in clinical care, and to prepare parents to provide the care their babies will need when released from the hospital.

## EDUCATION

University of Michigan, 2000
Ann Arbor, MI
Master of Science in Nursing with a minor in Education

University of Michigan, 1997
Ann Arbor, MI
Bachelor of Science in Nursing

## WORK EXPERIENCE

Providence Children's Hospital, 2000 to Present
Indianapolis, IN
Position: Staff Nurse
✛ Create and execute media presentations for parents of special care infants.
✛ Perform special nursing skills associated with caring for intensive care infants.

University of Michigan Medical Center, 1997 to 2000
Ann Arbor, MI
Position: Staff Nurse
✛ Devised new organizational structure to accommodate expanded ward.
✛ Acted as role model for new trainees receiving on-the-job training.

## REFERENCES

Available upon request

# Robert J. Zimmerman

Bob.Zimmerman@xxx.com

3897 Washington Blvd.
Noblesville, IN 46620
(317) 555-3467

## Career Goal

To obtain a position as a medical illustrator

## Education

**M.A., Medical Illustration in Art**
September 2000 - June 2003
University of San Diego
San Diego, CA
GPA 3.74
> Courses include drawing, layout, photography, illustration techniques, zoology, physiology, chemistry, biology, and histology.

**B.S., Zoology**
September 1995 - June 2000
University of Arizona
Tucson, AZ
Overall GPA 3.53
Major GPA 3.8
> Undergraduate courses included a strong concentration of science with an emphasis on art.

## Experience

*Noblesville Topic* Daily Newspaper
Noblesville, IN
1995 - 2000 (summers)
> Duties: worked in the illustration department at a variety of tasks and in the layout design department.

## References

Available upon request

# PETER MICHAEL JENNINGS, M.D.

114 LAUREL LANE • JAMESTOWN, PA 15904
P.JENNINGS99@XXX.COM • (314) 555-7874

## PRESENT PROJECT

Private practice in family medicine with special interest in critical care management.

## BACKGROUND

| | |
|---|---|
| 7/00 to 9/01 | Fellow, Department of Critical Care Medicine<br>Community Hospital, Pittsburgh, PA |
| 10/98 to 6/00 | Fellow, Department of Family Medicine<br>Temple University Hospital, Philadelphia, PA |
| 7/97 to 9/98 | Resident, PGY III Internal Medicine<br>Valley Memorial Hospital, Jamestown, PA |
| 7/96 to 7/97 | Resident, PGY II Internal Medicine<br>Valley Memorial Hospital, Jamestown, PA |
| 7/95 to 6/96 | Resident, PGY I Internal Medicine<br>Valley Memorial Hospital, Jamestown, PA |
| 5/95 to 6/95 | Assistant Resident, Internal Medicine<br>Valley Memorial Hospital, Jamestown, PA |
| 7/94 to 1/95 | Attended the Stanley Kaplan Educational Center, Houston, TX<br>Undertook an extensive self-guided study of basic and clinical sciences. |

## BACKGROUND (CONTINUED)

7/93 to 6/94   Rotating Resident Internship
Brown Memorial Hospital, Dallas, TX

9/88 to 5/93   Bachelor of Medicine and Bachelor of Surgery
Christian Medical College, Dallas, TX

## AFFILIATIONS

Associate Member, American College of Physicians

## LICENSURE

- Commonwealth of Pennsylvania, MD-55555555-L, DEA-55555555

- Board Certified in Internal Medicine by American Board of Internal Medicine, September 1998

- Board Eligible in Family Medicine by American Board of Internal Medicine

- Board Eligible in Critical Care Medicine

# Jennifer Bauer

*93 West 4th Street*
*Long Beach, CA 90808*
*E-mail: Jenny.Bauer@xxx.com*
*Home: (213) 555-9876*

## Education

Bachelor of Science in Cytotechnology, June 2000, GPA 3.65
California Institute of Technology
Pasadena, California

Relevant Courses:
♦ bacteriology
♦ physiology
♦ anatomy
♦ histology
♦ embryology
♦ zoology
♦ genetics
♦ chemistry
♦ computer classes

## Work Experience

Cytotechnologist
June 2000 - present
Circle Center Research Laboratory, Culver City, CA

♦ Duties include identifying cell specimens collected by fine needle aspiration and reporting findings to the pathologist.
♦ Use computers to measure cells, a new technique that is being developed at Circle Center Research Laboratory.

## Certification

♦ The International Academy of Cytology
♦ National Certification Agency for Medical Laboratory Personnel

## Honors

Dean's Honor List - Six Semesters

# CURRICULUM VITAE

## JASON L. PEABODY, M.D. F.A.C.P.

**Work Address**
> Department of Dermatology
> James R. Wright University, School of Medicine
> 690 N. Holland Street
> Lexington, KY 40292
> Telephone: (502) 555-9820

**Home Address**
> 8902 Douglas Drive
> Lexington, KY 40292
> Telephone: (502) 555-8753
> E-mail: Dr.Peabody@xxx.com

**Academic Title**
> Assistant Clinical Professor
> Department of Dermatology
> James R. Wright University
> School of Medicine

**Colleges and Universities Attended**
- B.A., Northwestern University, Evanston, IL – 1975
- M.D., Indiana University of Medicine, Indianapolis, IN – 1979

**University or Hospital Appointments**
> Rotating Intern, 1979 – 1980
> University of Oregon Health Sciences Center
> Portland, OR
>
> Residency in Dermatology, 1980 – 1982
> University of Oregon, Health Sciences Center
> Portland, OR
>
> Fellowship, Dermatology, 1982 – 1983
> University of Oregon, Health Sciences Center
> Portland, OR

**University or Hospital Appointments (Continued)**
    Associate Professor of Medicine, 1983 – 1995
    University of Oregon, Health Sciences Center
    Portland, OR

    Professor of Medicine, 1995 – present
    James R. Wright University School of Medicine
    Lexington, KY

**Board Certification**
- American Board of Dermatology, 1982
- American Board of Dermatopathology, 1984

**Licensure**
- Kentucky    (#5555555)
- Washington    (inactive)
- Oregon    (inactive)
- Indiana    (#55555555)

**Professional Societies**
- American Academy of Dermatology
- American Society of Dermatologic Surgery
- American Medical Association
- American Society of Dermatopathology

**Committees**
- Residency Review Committee, 1981 – 1982
- Pharmacy Committee, 1981 – 1982
- Research and Development Safety Subcommittee, 1986
- Private Practice Plan, 1987
- Research, 1989

**Committees (Continued)**

Oregon
- HMO-PPO Liaison Committee, 1992
- Clinical Computing, 1993

Lexington, KY
- Steering, Medical Outcomes, 1996
- Residency Evaluation Committee, 1997

**Elected National Positions**
- American Academy of Dermatopathology Board of Directors, 1992–1995
- Chairman, Annual Scientific Assembly, 1993
- Reelected to Board, March 1997
- Chair, Data Management Committee

**Grant Support**

Medical Research Foundation of Oregon
Travenol Laboratory
Upjohn Pharmaceutical Company
School of Medicine (University of Lexington)
Miles Laboratory
Department of Medicine (Oregon)

# ANN GOEBLE

**666 Central Avenue • Bay City, IN 46200**
**A.Goeble@xxx.com • (219) 555-8972**

| | |
|---|---|
| **JOB OBJECTIVE** | To provide quality nutritional care to individuals in nursing homes. |
| **EXPERIENCE**<br>**July 2002 - Present** | **Consultant**<br>**Sunset Manor Nursing Home**<br>**Indianapolis, IN**<br>• Develop standards for nutritional care.<br>• Conduct routine clinical duties.<br>• Work as a team member with patients and physicians to build up undernourished patients. |
| **June 1994 - July 2002** | **Dietetic Assistant**<br>**Broadmoor Nursing Home**<br>**Indianapolis, IN**<br>• Worked under dietetic supervisor in helping with menu planning, standardization of recipes, and the ordering of ingredients and supplies.<br>• Assisted patients with menu selections, and wrote basic modified dietary plans for patients. |
| **MEMBERSHIPS** | American Dietetic Association |
| **EDUCATION** | University of Indianapolis<br>Indianapolis, IN 46200<br>1990 - 1994<br>Degree: B.S. in Dietetics |
| **REFERENCES** | Upon request |

# MICHELLE A. HARMON

339 Lexington Place • Carmel, IN 46032
Home: (317) 555-8962 • Cellular: (317) 555-4329
E-mail: michelle.harmon@xxx.com

## OBJECTIVE

*To work on a health and research team as a Biomedical Engineer.*

## EDUCATION

**Purdue University**
Bachelor of Science, Biomedical Engineering, June 1998

### Related Course Work
- Biomedical Engineering
- Biomedical Computers
- Engineering Biophysics
- Bioinstrumentation
- Biomechanics
- Biotransport
- Artificial Organs

## EXPERIENCE

**Butler Williams Inc.**
**Indianapolis, IN**
**Bioengineer**
**1998 to Present**

Apply engineering principles to understanding the structure, function, and pathology of the human body. Also, use engineering concepts and technology to advance the understanding of biological, non-medical systems, such as maintaining and improving the quality of the environment and protecting human, animal, and plant life from toxicants and pollutants.

## AFFILIATIONS

The International Certification Commission

## REFERENCES

Available upon request

*CURRICULUM VITAE*

# SCOTT M. FRANK, M.D.

## PERSONAL DATA

**E-mail**              ScottFrank@xxx.com

**Home Address**        983 Crestview Drive
                        Osceola, IN 46544
                        (219) 555-9872

## EDUCATION

| Year | Degree | Institution |
|------|--------|-------------|
| 1987 | B.S. | University of Cincinnati |
| 1992 | M.D. | University of Cincinnati College of Medicine |

## POSTGRADUATE TRAINING

| Year | Position | Institution |
|------|----------|-------------|
| 1992-1995 | Residency<br><br>Norfolk, VA | East Virginia Graduate School of Medicine |
| 1995-1997 | Fellow, Nephrology<br><br>Troy, IA | University of Iowa Hospitals and Clinics |

## PROFESSIONAL EXPERIENCE

| Year | Position | Institution |
|------|----------|-------------|
| 1997-Present | Private Practice in Nephrology, Dialysis, and Transplantation | 8978 Foxworth, Suite 555 Osceola, IN 46244 |

## APPOINTMENTS

Medical Director: Dialysis
Osceola Medical Center - Osceola, IN
September 2001

Clinical Assistant Professor, Department of Internal Medicine
University of Osceola - Osceola, IN
January 2001

## COMMITTEES

Pharmacy and Therapeutics, Osceola Medical Center
Member, 1993-1996
Chair, 1996-Present

Institutional Review Board
Osceola Medical Center
Member, 1994-1996

Capital Equipment
Osceola Medical Center
Member, 1996-Present

## CERTIFICATIONS AND LICENSURE

### Certification
American Board of Internal Medicine - 3/26/92 - #55555
Nephrology, American Board of Internal Medicine - 11/11/92 - #555555

### Licensure (current)
Indiana - 7/2/92 - #555555

# Robin Peters

*90 Pacific Coast Highway • Malibu, CA 90024*
*(310) 555-3546 • Robin.Peters@xxx.com*

**Objective:**

To obtain a position with an ambulance company, hospital emergency room, or search and rescue team.

**Education:**

Santa Rosa Junior College, Santa Rosa, CA
Emergency Medical Technician Course 1A
Fire Service/Auto Extrication, 12/2000

Sonoma State University, Rohnert Park, CA
B.A., Environmental Studies, 1/2000
Included course work in Advanced First Aid, Emergency Care, Physiology, and Psychology.

**Experience:**

Sonoma Life Support, Sonoma, CA
Assisted paramedics and other EMTs on an ambulance as part of EMT certification, 11/2000

Emergency room, Santa Rosa Hospital, Santa Rosa, CA
Helped doctors and nurses in patient care as part of EMT certification, 10/2000

Home Care Program, Sonoma, CA
Nurse assistant for the elderly, 1999

Marine Conservation Corps, San Rafael, CA
Acted as corps member and driver, summer 1996–98

**Personal Qualifications:**

Excellent knowledge of medical terms.
Calm in emergency situations.
Polite, helpful, and compassionate.

**License and Certificate:**

Red Cross Community CPR Certificate - 2000
Red Cross Advanced First Aid - 1998

**Affiliations:**

National Parks Conservation Association
Sierra Club

**References:**

Available

| | |
|---|---|
| **Name:** | **Maria Black** |
| **Address:** | 1419 Cedar Drive<br>Dayton, OH 45226 |
| **Phone:** | (513) 555-8754 |
| **E-mail:** | Maria.Black@xxx.com |
| **Qualifications:** | Bachelor of Science in Pharmacy, 2002 |
| **School of Pharmacy:** | Dayton University |
| **Special Award:** | Merrell Dow Dayton School of Pharmacy's<br>Annual Award for Excellence, 2001 |
| **Previous Experience:** | Hooks Pharmacy, Summer Student<br>Dayton, OH<br>10 weeks, 2002 |
| | Royal Hospital, Summer Student<br>Dayton, OH<br>8 weeks, 2001 |
| | Ohio Drug, Saturday Staff<br>Dayton, OH<br>1996 - 2001 |
| **Present Position:** | Pharmacy Graduate Intern Program<br>Dayton Community Hospital<br>Dayton, OH |
| **Professional Interests:** | Clinical Pharmacy |
| **References:** | Available upon request |

# Peggy Martin

580 East Main St.  • Noblesville, IN 46210
Peg.Martin@xxx.com  • (344) 555-7690

## Education

Bachelor of Science, Pharmacy
Butler University, Indianapolis, IN
2000

## Previous Experience

**Gillian Griffiths Chemists Ltd., 2000 - present**
187 High Street
Indianapolis, IN 46208

Assistant Manager, responsible for two stores
2000 - 2002

Pharmacist
2002 - Present

**Hilton Drug Company, 1995 - 2000**
41 High Street
Indianapolis, IN 46208

Pre-registration experience and Assistant Manager
1995 - 1996

Relief Manager
1996 - 1998

Manager
1998 - 2000

## Additional Training

MRPTG courses including:
- Developing Management Skills
- Security in the Pharmacy
- First Aid

## References

As can be seen from the previous page, I have gained extensive experience in varied retail pharmacy outlets. I enjoy responsibility, possess good organizational skills, and get along well with people, both within the profession and with the general public. In support of this, I offer the following reference:

Luke P. Schmidt
Chief Pharmacist
Indiana Department of Public Welfare
449 Douglas Street
Noblesville, IN 46210
Phone: (317) 555-9000
E-mail: L.Schmidt@xxx.com


I will supply further references if requested.

# Eric M. Jefferson, M.D.
## — Curriculum Vitae —

**Office Address**
Martin Laboratory of Clinical Research
St. Ann's Hospital
Indianapolis, IN 46202
(317) 555-9871

**Home Address**
9802 Allen Lane
Carmel, IN 46032
Ejefferson@xxx.com
(317) 555-8466

## EDUCATION & TRAINING

B.S., Oregon State University, 1981

M.S. (Biochemistry), University of Oregon
Medical School, 1983

M.D. (cum laude), University of Oregon
Medical School, 1987

- Internship (general medicine), 7/87-7/90
- Residency (internal medicine), 7/91-7/94
Indiana University Medical School
Indianapolis, IN

- Fellowship (medical oncology), 7/88-7/90
- Fellowship (clinical pharmacology), 7/91-7/94
National Cancer Institute
National Institute of Health
Pittsburgh, PA

## ACADEMIC APPOINTMENTS

- Clinical Pharmacologist (8/99-present)
Martin Laboratory for Clinical Research

- Assistant Professor of Medicine (9/87-4/90)
- Assistant Professor of Pharmacology (2/87-4/90)
- Associate Professor of Medicine (4/90-present)
- Associate Professor of Pharmacology (4/90-present)
Indiana University Medical School, Indianapolis, IN

## CONSULTANTSHIPS

Consultant in Oncology
Indiana University Medical School

## SPECIALTY BOARD STATUS

Diplomate, National Board of Medical Examiners
Cert. #555555, 1987

Diplomate, National Board of Medical Oncology
Cert. #555555, 1987

## LICENSURE AND CERTIFICATION

State of Pennsylvania, #555-R, 1990
State of Indiana, #5555-L, 1990

## PROFESSIONAL SOCIETIES

- Member, American Federation for Clinical Research
- Fellow, American College of Physicians
- Member, C.G. Hangley Institute of Bloomington

## HONORS

- Phi Eta Sigma, 1980
- Phi Kappa Phi, 1981
- Alpha Omega Alpha, 1981

## TEACHING ASSIGNMENTS DURING PAST TWO YEARS

Ward Attending Staff, Medicine Service, St. Ann's Hospital, 1 month per year

Duties included supervising and teaching of house staff and medical students on clinical clerkships, and attending staff responsibility for medicine in-service patients.

## TEACHING ASSIGNMENTS (CONT.)

Consultant in Oncology, St. Ann's Hospital, 1 month per year

Duties included supervising fellows in medical oncology, teaching senior medical students on elective rotation, and formulating treatment plans for inpatients with cancer. Fellowship mentor—clinical pharmacology/medical oncology.

## PROFESSIONAL ACTIVITIES

Martin Research Committee Assignments:
• Oncology Action Group (new oncolytics selection)
• Oncology Strategy Working Group

## SERVICES

University Service—Member, Biostatistics Study and Planning Committee for four years (Dr. June Reasonor, chair).

Patient Care Service—Approximately 10% of time spent as responsible physician in charge of the oncology patients on the Martin Clinic Service at St. Ann's Hospital. Duties include direct primary patient care of 5-10 cancer patients in advanced state of their disease. Twelve months of the year.

Public Service—In April 1992, participated in an intensive one-week medical mission to the rural people of Haiti, sponsored by the national organization Lifeline and the Northside Christian Church of Indianapolis.

- ## *Roberta J. Stewart*

*34 King Crossing*
*Denver, CO 80203*
*(303) 555-1566*
*R.Stewart@xxx.com*

- ## *Career Objective*

Desire a position in office management in a medical or dental clinic.

- ## *Education*

Denver Technical College
Denver, CO – 1987
Completed Dental Assistant/Receptionist Program

Denver Community College
Denver, CO – 2001
Completed courses in WordPerfect, Lotus 1-2-3, Medical Office Management

- ## *Experience*

Denver Dental Clinic, 1993 – Present
124 Aspen Way, Denver, CO 80215
Office Manager
Handle office payroll and all billing for three dentists.
Deal with insurance forms.
Keep appointment book.

Dr. Leroy Atkins, 1988 – 1993
470 Rocky Mountain Drive, Boulder, CO 80217
Receptionist
Kept appointment book and updated records.

Dr. Thomas Marks, 1987 – 1988
85 Rocky Mountain Drive, Denver, CO 80217
Dental Assistant
Assisted the dentist at chairside and in the lab.
Took x-rays.
Prepared patients for oral surgery.

REFERENCES AVAILABLE

# ROSEMARIE JOHNSON

232 Lee Street      Durham, NC 27707      (919) 555-6541


**OBJECTIVE**          To become a member of the medical staff in a small clinic.


**EXPERIENCE**         *Registered Nurse*
                       **Durham Blood Bank, Durham, NC**
                       **1999 to present**
                       Draw blood, work with autologous program, and take charge
                       of unit when supervisor is absent.

                       *Private Duty Nurse*
                       **The Beck Agency, Durham, NC**
                       **1996 to 1999**
                       Provided long-term care in private homes.

                       *Floor Nurse*
                       **Durham General Hospital, Durham, NC**
                       **1995 to 1996**
                       Floor nurse in premature delivery.


**EDUCATION**          Bachelor of Science in Nursing, University of North Carolina,
                       1994

                       Refresher Courses, Durham General Hospital, 1994 to 2002
                       ➤ Care of Premature Infants
                       ➤ Infant Nutrition
                       ➤ Behavior Modification
                       ➤ Addictive Behaviors


**CERTIFICATION**      Certified as Registered Nurse, North Carolina, 1999


**REFERENCES**         Furnished on request

# PETER SIMMONS

678 Park Street                              Pete.Simmons@xxx.com
Portland, OR 97281                              (503) 555-4527

## OBJECTIVE

To obtain an executive position in marketing with a major pharmaceutical company dedicated to the research and development of new drugs.

## EXPERIENCE

**5/00 to Present**
**Coast Pharmaceuticals**
**Portland, OR**

**Duties**
Design marketing strategies for local and national markets.
Improved company's sales by over 15% during the last year.
Developed successful marketing program for generic drugs.

**1/99 to 5/00**
**Crestmore Laboratories**
**New York, NY**

**Achievements**
Set regional sales record in six months.
Exceeded company goals for the 1994 fiscal year.
Developed sales marketing program for the northwest region.

## EDUCATION

1998     M.B.A., UCLA, with concentration in Marketing
         Dean's List for six quarters

1996     B.A., University of Oregon, Business major
         G.P.A. was 3.8/4.0

REFERENCES AVAILABLE

# Maria Sanchez

285 Spruce Street
Pittsburgh, PA 19103
Maria.Sanchez@xxx.com
(412) 555-7896

## Experience

Full-time Nursing Assistant, 6/01 to Present
Water's Edge Convalescent Hospital, Pittsburgh, PA
• Involved in the personal care of geriatric patients.
• Assist with personal needs.
• Take blood pressure and temperature, check respiration rates.

Part-time student in nursing assistant program, 9/98 to 6/01
Mercy Hospital, Pittsburgh, PA

Teacher, 9/95 to 5/98
Douglas MacArthur High School
Manila, Philippines

## License

Certified Nurse Assistant, 2001
Pennsylvania, PA

## Reference

Susan Graves, Administrator
Water's Edge Convalescent Hospital
Pittsburgh, PA 15201
(412) 555-9122
Sue.Graves@xx.com

# ANDREW FISHER

82 South Twelfth Street • Grand Rapids, MI 49503
(616) 555-2983 • Andy.Fisher@xxx.com

## EXPERIENCE

My current position is medical record technician at the
Hillside Nursing Home, a 175-bed skilled care nursing facility in
Grand Rapids where I have worked for three years. My primary
responsibility is auditing medical records to make sure the
staff has carried out doctors' orders.

My previous job was at the Nimitz Navy Hospital in Detroit where
I worked for two years as a medical record technician putting together
patients' records after they left the hospital.

## EDUCATION

I graduated from Grand Rapids High School in the
top 20 percent of my class in 1998.

## REFERENCES

Personal and professional references are available
and will be submitted on request.

# CHRISTINE K. ROCK

15 Albert Lane
Vancouver, British Columbia V5Y IV4
Canada
CK.Rock@xxx.com
(604) 555-8963

## QUALIFICATIONS

- Pharmacy Degree (4 years)
- Advanced Resuscitation Award SSRL
- Award of Merit SSRL
- Duke of Edinburgh Award
- Completed 3rd year of BSC honors

## JOB OBJECTIVE

To use my pharmacy, communication, and organizational skills in a challenging position as a hospital pharmacist.

## STANDARD/FURTHER EDUCATION

1999 - 2003
University of British Columbia
Vancouver, British Columbia
Bachelor of Science, Pharmacy

1993 - 1999
Victoria High School
Vancouver, British Columbia

## SUBJECTS STUDIED

- Fundamentals of Pharmacology
- Pharmaceutical Chemistry I - V
- Pharmacy Practice
- Biopharmaceutics and Drug Disposition
- Drugs and Disease
- General Practice of Pharmacy
- Statistics
- Pharmaceutics 1
- Physiology I and II

## SUBJECTS STUDIED (CONT.)

- Physical Organic and Inorganic Chemistry
- Interpersonal Skills
- Bioscience
- Pharmaceutical Science and Drug Development
- Applications and Implications of Computers
- Marketing for Pharmacists

## PREVIOUS EXPERIENCE

July 2002 - September 2002
Rupert Group Research Limited
Assisted researchers in well-respected community pharmacy laboratory.
Gained experience operating drug analysis equipment.

July 2002
Prince Edward Hospital
Assigned to follow a tutor for a week, thus being involved in all aspects of hospital pharmacy.

June 2000 - June 2002
Fraser Pharmacy
Vacation and Saturday work
Involved in all aspects of a community pharmacy.
Dealt with customers at medicine and cosmetic counters.
Prepared and endorsed prescriptions.

December 1999 - June 2002
Vancouver Regional Council
Activity Specialist (Lifeguard) at a Local Youth Club.
Carried out safety precautions and instructed staff in the proper use of equipment.

June 1998 - September 1998
Rosedale District Council
Lifeguard
Supervised public swimming at an outdoor pool.

## REFERENCES

Available upon request

# EVAN L. WATERFIELD

1254 PLAZA DRIVE
YOUNGSTOWN, OH 44512
EVAN.WATERFIELD@XXX.COM
(216) 555-8989

## EDUCATION

June 1996 to January 1998
Ohio Vocational Schools, Inc.
Youngstown, OH
Completed practical nursing program.

## EXPERIENCE

SLEEPY HOLLOW NURSING HOME
45 DIAMOND LANE
YOUNGSTOWN, OH 44513

DIRECTOR OF STAFF DEVELOPMENT, FEBRUARY 2000 TO PRESENT
Interview new patients and their families, review facility patient care plan and revise when necessary, orient new staff, give in-service workshops for staff to update knowledge of equipment, medicine, and changes in facility.

STAFF NURSE, FEBRUARY 1998 TO JANUARY 2000
Passed medicines, gave treatments, and provided basic nursing care.

## LICENSE

Licensed Practical Nurse: Ohio license #5555

REFERENCES AVAILABLE

# PETRA LEVENTHAL

109 Beach Drive ✦ Virginia Beach, VA 23456 ✦ (804) 555-9852 ✦ P.Leventhal@xxx.com

## OBJECTIVE
To secure a teaching position at a major medical school.

## WORK STYLE
- ✦ Specialist in resolving eating disorders
- ✦ Skilled in adapting counseling to client
- ✦ Analytic and versatile thinker
- ✦ Communicate with clients and parents with warmth and diplomacy

## EXPERIENCE
Clinical Psychologist
Alta Vista Hospital, Virginia Beach, VA
1998 to Present
- ✦ Established an eating disorder clinic
- ✦ Counseled over 100 teenagers with eating disorders
- ✦ Initiated peer counseling program
- ✦ Developed intern program
- ✦ Created a program to assess which clients would require hospitalization

University of Virginia
1998 - academic year
- ✦ Taught class on eating disorders
- ✦ Received psychology department's "Excellence in Teaching Award"

## EDUCATION
Ph.D. in Psychology, University of Virginia, 1998
Concentration: eating disorders

M.S. in Psychology, Yale University, 1996

B.A. in Psychology, Georgetown University, 1994
Graduated magna cum laude

## AFFILIATIONS
- ✦ Virginia Association of Psychologists, secretary
- ✦ American Association of Psychologists
- ✦ Eating Disorder Association of America

# VICTORIA MARIE HOOPER

*4687 Braewick Drive*
*Indianapolis, IN 46236*
*vicky_hooper@xxx.com*
*(317) 555-0963*

## Job Objective

Seeking a full-time position as a registered nurse with eventual entry into a management position.

## Education

B.S., Nursing, 1990
Salve Regina College
Newport, RI

## Skills and Abilities

### Public Relations

- People-oriented
- Chair/coordinator for several health fairs
- Health risk assessment coordinator
- Health related counseling screening

### Management

- Eleven years as navy nurse managing subordinates including corps members and junior nurses
- Chair of hospital/nursing related committees
- Charge nurse in multifaceted family practice clinic
- Dual role as nursing education/patient education coordinator

## Work Experience

Commissioned
November 1990
Navy Nurse Corps

Staff Nurse: Orthopedics, Pediatrics, and ICU/RR
December 1990 to February 1994
Great Lakes Naval Hospital

*Page 1 of 2*

## Work Experience (continued)

Staff Nurse, Medicine Assistant Charge Nurse: Pediatrics
March 1994 to November 1997
Jacksonville Naval Hospital

Staff Nurse: Pediatric Acute Care Clinic
November 1997 to June 1999
Portsmouth Navy Hospital

Staff Nurse: Medical Surgical
June 1999 to August 1999
Orlando Naval Hospital

Charge Nurse
August 1999 to August 2000
Family Practice Clinic

Nursing Education/Patient Education Coordinator
August 2000 to December 2001

Honorable Discharge from United States Navy
December 15, 2001

Engaged in job search
December 2001 to January 2002

Health Nurse
Fort Benjamin Harrison Community Hospital
March 2002 to present

References Available

# Pennie Cole Jones

80 Chestnut Street
Minneapolis, MN 55416
Home: (612) 555-8461
Work: (612) 555-3932

Physical Therapy License: Minnesota #55555

## Employment Experience

**August 1995 to Present**
Specializing in outpatient neurological and orthopedic diagnoses
Co-owner of Physical Therapy Associates of St. Louis Park
400 Lakeshore Drive
St. Louis Park, MN 55417

**October 1993 to August 1995**
Acute Rehabilitation, Staff Therapist
Bloomington Memorial Hospital
Bloomington, MN 55439

**August 1991 to October 1993**
Physical Therapy Aide
Minneapolis Rehabilitation Center
Minneapolis, MN 55419

**August 1989 to August 1991**
Physical Therapy Aide
Crestwood Rehabilitation Hospital
Rochester, MN 56214

## Professional Education

B.S. Degree in Physical Therapy, 1989
University of California, Santa Barbara

B.A. Degree in Pre-Physical Therapy, minor in Psychology, 1986
California State University, Turlock

# Continuing Education

**April 1994**
NDT for Adult Hemiplegia Certification Course

**October 1994**
Traumatic Brain Injury Conference

**October-April, 1998-1999**
Myofascial Strategies I

**May-November, 1999**
Myofascial Strategies II

**February 2000**
New Treatments for Lower Back Pain

**October 2000**
The Active Foot Symposium

**December 2001**
Cranio-Sacral I


REFERENCES AVAILABLE

# MARK JOHNSON

971 Gable Street • Boca Raton, FL 33431
(407) 555-8765 • M.Johnson@xxx.com

## WORK HISTORY

2001-present
Clear Speech
Boca Raton, FL
*Speech-language pathologist*
• Evaluation, diagnosis, and treatment of children with speech
  disorders.

2000-2001
Santa Clara County School for the Deaf
San Jose, CA
*Speech-language pathologist and sign language instructor*
• Taught students and family the fundamentals of sign language.

1999-2000
Private Practice
Chicago, IL
• Specialized in screening of preschoolers for early identification
  of hearing and speech impaired.

1996-1999
Chicago Public Schools
Chicago, IL
*Speech-language pathologist*
• Elementary School District: Early identification of hearing and
  speech impaired (one year).
• High School District: Treatment of mentally and physically
  impaired students with speech problems and learning disabled
  students with ESL (one year).

# EDUCATION

1996
Northwestern University
Chicago, IL
M.A., Speech Pathology

1994
University of Wisconsin
Madison, WI
B.A., Arts and Sciences with Speech and Hearing specialty

# CERTIFICATION

Certificate of Clinical Competence of the American Speech and Hearing Association

# PROFESSIONAL AFFILIATIONS

- American Speech and Hearing Association
- Florida Speech and Hearing Association
- Greater Boca Raton Speech and Hearing Association

# SPECIAL QUALIFICATIONS

Fluent at signing

*References on request*

# Rita Garden

32 Elliott Avenue

Austin, TX 78731

(512) 555-5618

## Career Objective

To become a regional administrator in a large nursing home corporation.

## Employment Highlights

Six years of experience in the administration of nursing homes in Austin, Texas. Acted as administrator in facilities ranging from 60 beds to 175 beds, and in intermediate and skilled care nursing homes.

## Experience

1999-Present
Austin Nursing Homes, Inc., Austin, TX
2000: Promoted to Administrator, Desert Valley Home
1999-2000: Assistant Administrator, Desert Valley Home

1997-1999
Goodwin Nursing Homes, Inc., Austin, TX
1999: Administrator, Austin Convalescent Hospital, Alzheimer's Unit
1998: Administrator, Southwest Nursing Home
1997: Assistant Administrator, Southwest Nursing Home

## Education

June 1997
B.S. in Health Science (summa cum laude)
University of Texas, Austin, TX

## Certification

June 1997
Nursing Home Administrator, License #5555

References on Request

# Chapter 6

# *Sample Cover Letters*

This chapter contains many sample cover letters for people pursuing a wide variety of jobs and careers in the fields of health and medicine, or who have had experience in these fields in the past.

There are many different styles of cover letters in terms of layout, level of formality, and presentation of information. These samples also represent people with varying amounts of education and work experience. Choose one cover letter or borrow elements from several different cover letters to help you construct your own.

1090 Oak Drive
Madison, WI 54702

January 14, 20—


Mercy Hospital
6225 Maple Drive
Indianapolis, IN 46220

To Whom It May Concern:

This letter is in response to the advertisement for an emergency medical technician that appeared in the *Indianapolis News* last Friday evening. Please accept my resume in consideration for this position.

With a degree from the University of Wisconsin and five years of work experience as a medical technician at Community North Hospital in Madison, Indiana, I believe that I am suited to your hospital's needs.

Thank you for your time and consideration. I look forward to hearing from you soon.

Sincerely,


Martin A. Gordon
(715) 555-8954

Enclosure

# KATHERINE MALLOY

510 PINE STREET • SAN RAMON, CA 94542
(510) 555-5642

February 8, 20—

Dr. Elena Rodriguez
50 Central Avenue
Danville, CA 94526

Dear Dr. Rodriguez:

Thank you for speaking with me yesterday about the dental hygienist opening in your office. After talking with you and learning more about your office and philosophy, I feel more confident than ever that my skills would benefit you and your staff. With my extensive experience and outstanding education and training, I believe that I would be an asset to your office. I am enclosing a copy of my resume to give you a better idea of my work history and would appreciate the opportunity to discuss it further with you in person.

Thank you for your time and consideration and I look forward to hearing from you at your earliest convenience.

Sincerely,

Katherine Malloy

# Dorothea P. Russell

*209 East Main Street*
*Philadelphia, PA 19103*
*(215) 555-9845*

March 25, 20—

Saint Vincent's Hospital
635 Medical Drive, Suite 248
Wilkes-Barre, PA 18711

Dear Sir/Madam:

I am interested in the position of psychiatric social worker, which you advertised in this Sunday's *Citizen Voice*. As you can see from the enclosed resume, I have considerable experience working with adult psychiatric patients in a variety of mental health care facilities, including the traditional hospital setting.

I would like the opportunity to meet with you to discuss my qualifications. I feel that I would be a productive addition to your hospital staff.

Sincerely,

Dorothea P. Russell

# *Margaret Morgan*

**3033 Diamond Drive • Indianapolis, IN 46220 • 317/555-1881**

November 8, 20—

Riley Children's Hospital
5892 Dupont Avenue
Indianapolis, IN 46256

Dear Sir/Madam:

I am responding to your ad in the *Indiana Times* for a neonatology instructor.

I am presently a graduate student at the Indiana University School of Nursing pursuing an advanced degree in Pediatric Nursing Education. I plan to graduate in June of next year with honors.

My resume is enclosed for your review. As you can see, I have extensive experience in the field of education and have further expanded my credentials to include specialization in the area of neonatology.

Riley Children's Hospital is the kind of well-respected and venerable institution that attracts me. The focus on patient care and well-being, in particular, is in alignment with my personal work philosophy. I strongly feel that my skills would be of benefit to Riley Children's Hospital.

Please contact me if you require additional information.

I look forward to hearing from you.

Sincerely,

Margaret Morgan

Enclosure

Anthony H. Cohen
167 Tuxedo Drive
Redding, CT 06896
(203) 555-1678

February 8, 20—

Mr. George Smart
Director of Personnel
Vocational Technical College
8775 West Douglas Street
Virginia Beach, VA 23456

Dear Mr. Smart:

For the past ten years, I have had a rewarding career with Central State Hospital in Connecticut. I now find myself ready to take on a new challenge as a teacher of mental health workers.

During my career at Central State Hospital, I have held positions as mental health counselor and director of psychiatric social work. Being part of the mental health community has shown me the great need for well-trained workers in this area.

I would like the opportunity to speak with you about my background and the potential areas where my expertise can be used to train mental health workers. The enclosed resume describes my qualifications.

I will call early next week to discuss your current needs and the possibility of meeting with you in person.

Sincerely yours,


Anthony H. Cohen

AHC/tbd

Enclosure

2234 Eden Hollow Road, Suite 5
New York, NY 10020
Office: (212) 555-7788
Home: (212) 555-0098


August 27, 20—

Mr. John Boyd
The Far West Pharmaceutical Company
7722 Oakwood Drive
San Ramon,CA 94527

Dear Mr. Boyd:

The progressive and innovative nature of the The Far West Pharmaceutical Company appeals to me.

I am looking for a position as a salesperson with a pharmaceutical house after spending the past five years as a pharmacist in a retail store.

A resume is enclosed that describes my experience and qualifications. I look forward to hearing from you soon to set up an appointment for an interview.

Please keep all contact personal and confidential.

Sincerely,


Michael K. Smith

# DAVID ALLEN CONNORS

5578 Douglas Drive                          Council Bluffs, Iowa 51504

October 19, 20—

Human Resources
Green Glen Assisted Living
825 North Woodland Drive
Council Bluffs, Iowa 51503

To Whom It May Concern:

I am writing to inquire about any openings you may have for clinical nurse specialists in geriatric medicine. My experience in geriatric nursing includes working in the Alzheimer's unit of Memorial Hospital and the Oak Brook Nursing Home.

Recently, I completed a Gerontological Nurse Practitioner training program. In addition, I hold gerontology certification.

If you should have an interest in further discussing my qualifications, please contact me at (712) 555-0134.

My resume is enclosed for your review.

Sincerely,

David Allen Connors

# Charles D. Stiles
6225 High Drive • New Brunswick, NJ 08901 • (201) 555-2609

October 8, 20—

Human Resources Department
Clear Laboratories
13 Aspen Drive
Trenton, NJ 06902

Dear Sir/Madam:

I am writing to you with the hope that you might have an opening soon in your laboratory for a medical technologist. If you do not, I would appreciate you keeping my resume on file for future opportunities.

I recently completed course work at Johns Hopkins for a Master's degree in Medical Technology. Presently, I am completing my research project in microbiology.

I am a sincere, hardworking individual with the ability to learn quickly. I enjoy challenging work and am capable of working under pressure.

Thank you for taking the time to consider my qualifications and candidacy. I look forward to hearing from you soon.

Sincerely yours,


Charles D. Stiles

Enclosure

# Maria P. Day

**3345 Lucas Street**
**Dallas, TX 75235**

January 19, 20—

Personnel Director
Washington Township School Corporation
93 Lindenwood Ave.
Austin, TX 78768

Dear Personnel Director:

I am writing to obtain further information regarding employment with your school corporation as a school nurse.

I read about your corporation in the *Texan State Journal* and would like to inquire about career opportunities within your school district.

I will be graduating from SMU in May of this year with a Bachelor of Science degree in Nursing. Throughout my collegiate career, I have maintained a balanced schedule of activities and academics. In addition, my summer internship provided invaluable work experience in the emergency room at Kennedy Hospital.

A copy of my resume is enclosed for your review. If you need further information, I will be more than happy to provide you with the necessary materials.

I know how busy you must be during this time of year, but I would appreciate a few minutes of your time. I may be reached at the above address or by calling (214) 555-2203. I look forward to hearing from you regarding my future with your school corporation.

Sincerely,


Maria P. Day

Enclosure: Resume

December 17, 20—


Ruth Fong
Pacific Press
255 Long Hill Rd.
Middletown, CT 06457

Dear Ms. Fong:

I wish to apply for a position as a medical illustrator with Pacific Press.

I hold an undergraduate degree in Biology and a Master's degree in Medical Illustration. In addition, I am a member of the Association of Medical Illustrators. I have an extensive and varied background working on ophthalmology drawings as well as with educators and authors. This experience, combined with my schooling and personal interest in illustrating, could be very valuable to your company.

Enclosed is my resume. I am willing to relocate. Please feel free to call me and set up an interview at your convenience.

Sincerely,


Jerome Palmer
5544 Wildwood Drive
West Lake, Ohio 44145
(614) 555-4014

# Edda Fisher

### 2556 Forest Street • Houston, TX 77063

January 27, 20—

Personnel Director
Valley Hospital
P.O. Box 228964
Birmingham, AL 35222-8964

Dear Personnel Director:

Please consider my application for a position as a dietitian. I graduated from Purdue University with a Bachelor of Science degree in Dietetics. I have been a registered dietitian for the past three years.

I feel that my experience as a dietitian in a nursing home and clinic, along with my education, qualifies me for a position with Valley Hospital. I will continue to be successful as a dietitian because I enjoy the challenge of helping people to regain their health through proper diet. Furthermore, I work hard and am concerned with doing my best at all times.

I would like to have an interview to discuss how my placement with your hospital would benefit both of us. Please phone me any time at (713) 555-8866. I look forward to hearing from you.

Yours truly,


Edda Fisher


Enclosure

November 21, 20—

Dr. James Day
Clay Hospital
9888 West Washington Blvd.
Indianapolis, In 46208

Dear Dr. Day:

This letter is in reply to the advertisement in the *Indianapolis Star* on Sunday, November 19 seeking a music therapist. I believe I am an excellent candidate for that position.

I earned a degree in Music Therapy from Indiana University in May of this year. Recently, I completed an internship at Coleman Hospital in Indianapolis where I worked with severely retarded children. I play the piano, guitar, violin, and recorder and enjoy using folk music as a part of my treatment therapy. I have attached a qualifications summary and other pertinent data for your consideration.

I think that my experiences can be utilized by Clay Hospital to your advantage, and I look forward to an interview with you.

Sincerely,


Kathy Johnson
1516 North Central Avenue
Indianapolis, IN 46208
(317) 555-3953

# JILL R. McCOY

473 Hill Drive West
Lincolnwood, IL 60646
(847) 555-6320

March 13, 20—

Ms. Julia Serafini
Crestwood Manor
6341 Crestwood Dr.
Naperville, IL 60565

Dear Ms. Serafini:

I will be graduating from Northwestern University in May. I am seeking a position as an occupational therapist in a nursing home setting.

My education at Northwestern University exposed me to the latest developments in occupational therapy. It also provided me with the opportunity to work with individuals in retirement communities, senior citizen centers, and rehabilitation centers. In addition, I have enhanced my education with extra courses in gerontology.

Enclosed, you will find my resume. A complete credentials file is available upon request through Northwestern University, Educational Placement Office; 4600 S. Main Street; Evanston, IL 60043; (847) 555-9987.

I would like to request an interview with Crestwood Manor. I may be contacted at the above number.

Sincerely,


Jill R. McCoy

Enclosure

Elizabeth A. Grossa
1346 E. 22nd St. #105
Chicago, IL 60302
(312) 555-9862

January 8, 20—

Optics Plus
8465 Baker Street
Chicago, IL 60302

To Whom It May Concern:

This letter is in response to the Optics Plus ad placed in the *Chicago Tribune* last Sunday.

I have a Master in Ophthalmic Optics certificate and hold an Illinois license to dispense eyeglasses. I have worked in a hospital eye clinic for seven years and would now like to work in a retail optical store. Your ad was of particular interest to me as the job is for a position in the Chicago area.

My experience in the hospital environment has given me the opportunity to handle a wide variety of vision needs. Besides being a skilled optician, I have been told that my communication skills are excellent.

My resume is enclosed, detailing my work experience, certification, and educational background. I feel that my qualifications would be an asset to your corporation.

I would welcome the opportunity for a personal interview to discuss the position at Optics Plus.

Sincerely,


Elizabeth A. Grossa

# GEORGE LONG

**655 Kelton Avenue**
**Los Angeles, CA 90024**
**(310) 555-9542**

December 4, 20—

Anita Johnson
Los Angeles Drug Company
500 South Summit Drive
Burbank, CA 95123

Dear Ms. Johnson:

Please accept this letter as an application for the position of manager of the prescription department in the Burbank branch of the Los Angeles Drug Company. I have enclosed a copy of my resume for your review.

Through my present employment as a pharmacist with Goldman Drugs, I have gained firsthand experience in merchandising, advertising, purchasing stock, and supervising pharmacists and clerks. My formal education also includes an undergraduate degree in Business. Furthermore, I possess the interpersonal skills and strong professional background that this position requires.

I would very much like to discuss my qualifications further in an interview.

Sincerely,


George Long

December 9, 20--

JOANNE POWERS
95 LOWELL DRIVE
KALAMAZOO, MI 49001
(616) 555-4889

Dr. Charlene Dixon
Kraft Medical Center
1000 Campus Drive
Kalamazoo, MI 49001

Dear Dr. Dixon:

I am responding to your advertisement in last Friday's *Gazette*.
I am interested in a full-time position as a receptionist/secretary
in your office.

Presently, I am working as a secretary in the office of Dr. Charles
Williams, who will be retiring at the end of this month. My experience with Dr. Williams has included billing, data entry, patient
scheduling, clerical work, and handling collection of patient
accounts.

I am a self-starter who is resourceful, outgoing, efficient, service-
oriented, and extremely organized. Superior recommendations
are available from my current employer.

I look forward to hearing from you in the near future to schedule an interview.

Yours truly,


Joanne Powers

Enclosure

ANGELA CASTLE
225 Landon Drive
Ionia, Michigan 49546
(616) 555-1053

November 12, 20—

Ralph Jansen, D.D.S.
1224 East Drive
Detroit, Michigan 48079

Dear Doctor Jansen,

Are you looking for someone who can:
• Play a key role in patient care?
• Work with children and adults in a gentle and caring manner?
• Effectively handle emergencies?
• Offer knowledge in areas such as dental implants and cosmetic bonding?
• Work on evenings and Saturdays?

In the ten years that I have worked as a dental assistant, I have assisted dentists in general dentistry as well as handled billing and appointments. In addition, I have experience with computer-aided dentistry. My experience has taught me the importance of good people skills and keeping abreast of the most recent technological advances in dentistry.

I look forward to the opportunity to meet with you personally to discuss my qualifications as a dental assistant. You may contact me in the evenings at the above telephone number.

Very truly yours,


Angela Castle

Enclosure

## *Michael R. Crowe*                                    May 21, 20—
*19 East 83rd Street, Apt. 32*
*New York, New York 10024*
*(212) 555-5626*

---

Ms. Linda Lansing
Director, Human Resources
New York General Hospital
78 Lexington Avenue
New York, New York 10028

Dear Ms. Lansing:

Please accept this letter and my resume as an application for a position on the New York General Hospital staff. As a compassionate, hardworking professional who is willing to put in long hours, I believe I can make a positive contribution to your hospital.

As you may note in my resume, I have recently completed my residency at Walter Reed Hospital in Washington, D.C. During my time at Walter Reed, I also worked as a volunteer three nights a week for the Homeless Help Program. Through my volunteer activities, I have gained experience working with a vast number of individuals of various ages and socioeconomic backgrounds.

Besides solid medical skills, you will find that I have exceptionally strong organizational skills and am able to work independently with little or no supervision. I am looking for a hospital where I can best utilize my personal and professional skills, and satisfy my desire to serve the community.

Should my qualifications meet the needs of your hospital, I would appreciate the opportunity for a personal interview at your earliest convenience. If you should need any additional information regarding my qualifications, please do not hesitate to contact me at any time.

Thank you for your time and consideration. I look forward to talking with you in the very near future.

Sincerely,


Michael R. Crowe

Encl: Resume, References

# Stephanie Kohl

3412 South York Avenue
Chicago, IL 61646
213-555-6321

January 23, 20—

Crystal Brown
250 Marquette Ave.
Minneapolis, MN 55401

Dear Ms. Brown:

I am seeking a position as a speech-language pathologist in an elementary school setting, and I am looking forward to relocating to the Greater Minneapolis area.

I received my Master's degree in Speech-Language Pathology from the University of Minnesota and hold state licenses in Illinois and Minnesota. My experience includes working in public elementary and secondary schools as well as at a county school for the hearing impaired. In addition, I sign fluently.

My resume is enclosed to assist you in evaluating my qualifications. If you need further information, please let me know.

I look forward to meeting with you to discuss your current staffing needs and my qualifications for employment in your school district. Thank you for your consideration.

Sincerely,

Stephanie Kohl